WITCHCRAFT

Ancient & Modern

Raymond Buckland

Queen Victoria Press

Copyright © 1970, 2017 Raymond Buckland

All rights reserved. No portion of this book may be reproduced without written permission from the publisher, except in the case of a reviewer who wishes to quote brief passages in connection with a review for inclusion in a magazine, newspaper, or journal.

Illustrations by Raymond Buckland

ISBN 978-0-9978481-8-2

CONTENTS

About the Author /

Introduction

PART I

Chapter
1. Give the Public What It Wants / 9
2. Stern Voices of Authority / 21
3. Actions Speak Louder Than Words / 37
4. Political Witchcraft? / 55
5. Old England . . . / 63
6. . . . New England / 73

PART II

7. Into Sharper Focus / 101
8. Spokes of the Wheel / 109
9. Ingredients of Witchcraft / 133
10. Horns But No Tail / 149
11. The Witch Alone / 164
12. "Let's All Cast Spells!" / 175
13. Ways of Witchcraft / 184

Bibliography / 191

Raymond Buckland

Raymond Buckland is an Englishman who made his home in the United States nearly 60 years ago, in 1962. Educated at King's College, London, England, he has been actively involved in the study of various aspects of the paranormal for well over seventy years. He is an internationally known, award winning author of more than 50 books, with titles translated into 17 foreign languages.

He has produced decks of tarot cards and other divination cards and tools, including the Buckland Spirit Board.

Raymond Buckland is regarded as one of the leading authorities on witchcraft, voodoo and the supernatural, and has served in an advisory capacity for Paramount Pictures and Twentieth Century Fox. He has appeared in movies, videos, on national and internatonal television, and been written about in many publications both in the United States and abroad.

His books may be seen at www. raymondbucklandbooks. com and at www. queenvictoriapress. com

PART I

Devil from Hearne's Print of
The "Descent Into Hell." 1676

There are two main ways of witchcraft, each quite different dependant upon your point of view. For hundreds of years just one of these views had held supreme—the view of the Church. Only in recent years (as recently as the last forty years) has the other view been presented . . . that of the witches themselves.

* * *

Since the very beginning of printing, in the late Middle Ages, virtually every book on the subject has told us that witchcraft was an evil; that witches were the servants of the Devil, working against Christendom. Witchcraft was apparently a product of the harsh Church of its time. It was a rebellion of the lower classes against the religious strictness of the Early Middle Ages. The peasant found that he could not better his lot by praying to a god who was always too busy with the rich, so why not pray to the Devil, if only to show disdain for his peers? The Devil did not do the peasant any good either, he found, but at least he had the satisfaction of knowing that he was "fighting the establishment"! He was protesting in the only way possible for him. Mother Church, aware of this protest, sought to crush it by force. The peasant had always been treated thus, and he must be made to like it.

Zealous bishops scurried hither and thither

keeping their priests on their toes, seeking out the dissenters. All the Devil-worshippers were to be brought to trial, shown the error of their ways, and punished. A book was drawn up to be used as a guide for those unfamiliar with the "disease" of witchcraft. Entitled the *Malleus Maleficarum* (Hammer of the Witches) it listed the many ways of recognizing a witch; the varieties of "persuasion" that could be employed to obtain the correct answers to the questions it listed; and the punishments felt to be most suitable for the miscreants when they were assuredly found guilty. With this book as a basis it was to become easy to fight the enemies of the Church.

Witchcraft, after a long bitter struggle, finally collapsed. With approximately nine million "enemy" killed Christianity was triumphant. The Church's views put forward on the ways of witchcraft had apparently been proven, and were to remain for the next few hundred years.

There certainly was an occasional dissenter—a writer who felt that the so-called witchcraft had been a great delusion. Indeed during the eighteenth century for a while it was fashionable to hold that the witches had held no special powers at all, that they did not really worship the Devil; in fact that the whole thing had been an illusion. Then came another group who violently disagreed. Witchcraft was precisely what the Church had said it to be—an emergence of the Devil, an effort to overthrow the true believers, a misleading of the gullible. As a reward for their evil-doings the Devil rewarded his followers with powers—to fly through the air, to raise storms, to kill through use of a wax figure.

These, then, were the ways of witchcraft as seen by the "average" man right through until the twentieth century, simply because they were the only ways shown to him. But in this twentieth century a new way was presented. A well-known scholar suggested that perhaps there was more to witchcraft than we had been led to believe. She suggested that it was actually the remains of a pre-Christian religion, stemming from the Stone Age. The reason it had been presented, by the Church, in the guise of a devilish uprising was because as an earlier religion it could be a dangerous rival. If they could not convert its followers then better by far to kill them.

Confirmation of this new view of the ways of witchcraft was not to come until as recently as 1951. Then, with the repeal of the old laws against witchcraft, actual witches started to tell their side of the story. Witchcraft was indeed an old religion, they said. It had *not* been killed, in the Middle Ages, but was still very much alive!

* * *

The first part of this book is going to go over the so-long-held ideas on witchcraft. To look through the eyes of the early Church and see the Devil and his servants working their evil ways. It will look at the persecutions, as they hysterically grew. It will look at actual trials of the Middle Ages—what was said and done . . . and why.

The second part of the book will then look out through the very eyes of the witches themselves. It will show where witchcraft actually started, how it developed, and why it was so misrepresented. In this latter part of the book will be found the rites of witchcraft *as they are still practised today*. The construction of the *covens* (groups of witches), the practises and beliefs. The true ways of witchcraft.

CHAPTER 1

GIVE THE PUBLIC WHAT IT WANTS

The dawning of the Age of Aquarius has brought with it a tremendous interest in all matters "occult". Not just for the younger people —for everyone. Books on astrology are today outselling all other subjects. Businessmen are having their horoscopes cast and making their business decisions according to the signs. Housewives are meeting for ouija-board and tarot-card afternoons rather than cards, coffee and scandal. High school students and college professors alike are looking a little more closely at the lines in the palms of their hands.

On to this scene burst, in 1967, a novel which only a year or so earlier would have been shuffled in amongst the gothics and nurse-romances and subsequently forgotten. The novel was called *Rosemary's Baby*, written by a man named Ira Levin.

With the growing interest in, and knowledge of, the various aspects of the supernatural this story, about a young couple who get involved in "witchcraft", was swiftly snapped up and avidly read and discussed. In no time at all a movie was made of it—setting some kind of a record in that the film script stuck closely to the book. "Witchcraft", albeit of the Ira Levin variety, was suddenly the IN thing.

* * *

On television had appeared a light-comedy series called *Bewitched*, starring the delightful Elizabeth Montgomery as a modern day house-wife-cum-witch named Samantha. She struggles valiantly with herself trying to do her housework the "normal" way, rather than giving in to the temptation of casting a swift spell to take care of everything. On the one side is her husband, trying to keep her like any other modern day housewife; on the other side is her mother, a traditional witch who zaps into and out of the domestic scene dispensing temptation left, right, and center.

Bewitched, much as its inspirator *Bell, Book and Candle*, has a very definite lightness. The witchcraft is a "fun" thing. No spells are cast that really hurt or injure anyone. There is no demonology, or Satanism, involved. The program enjoys great success, being watched by young and old alike and being enjoyed also by witches themselves—which is more than can be said for *Rosemary's Baby*.

* * *

"She . . . lay down, and was suddenly surrounded by naked men and women, ten or a dozen, with Guy among them. They were elderly, the women grotesque and slack-breasted. Minnie and her friend Laura-Louise were there, and

Roman in a black miter and a black silk robe. With a thin black wand he was drawing designs on her body, dipping the wand's point in a cup of red held for him by a sun-browned man with a white moustache. The point moved back and forth across her stomach and down ticklingly to the insides if her thighs. The naked people were chanting—flat, unmusical, foreign-tongued syllables—and a flute or clarinet accompanied them."

The Devil himself has intercourse with Rosemary and she finally begets his offspring, the Satanic Messiah. It is a frightening thought, yet one which seemed to capture the imagination of the general public. Perhaps it is for the same reason that people go to auto races hoping, deep down inside, that they will witness a bloody accident. For the same reason that people will flock to the scene of a murder—the bloodier the better.

There seems to be, in most of us, a deep inherent streak of sadism. A part of us that enjoys danger and horror. Frequently it has its masochistic tendencies—the identification of self with victim. For whatever the reason it is indisputable that the majority of people are fascinated by the horrific, by evil, by the idea of flirting with fate. All this together with the recent smattering of occult knowledge led to the success of *Rosemary's Baby*.

Rapidly so-called "covens of witches" sprang up all over the country. At last there was something to *do*; something different. Groups of friends could get together and, stripping naked, worship —perhaps "tempt" would be a better word—the Devil. The newly-learned arts of tarot card reading, palmistry, psychometry, could be incorporated as part of these rites.

So there are, so far, two possible ways of treating witchcraft both of them, on the face of it, quite valid. One is the innocuous style of *Bewitched*; the other is serious and—as will be seen —highly dangerous participation as in *Rosemary's Baby*. Which is the more correct way of witchcraft?

A popular English writer named Dennis Wheatley is all for the Ira Levin variety. Wheatley was writing black magic stories long before Levin even knew there was such a subject. Like Levin he happily mixes the ingredients of witchcraft, ceremonial magic, black magic and voodoo all in the same pot. Although actually quite separate and distinct subjects for the purposes of the novel they are, to these authors, merely an interchangeable variety of the same. Wheatley's description of a modern day witches; Sabbat sounds remarkably credible, for it is just as we could imagine it ourselves after reading of the Sabbats of the early Middle Ages:

"The two slit-eyes, slanting inwards and down, gave out a red baleful light. Long pointed ears cocked upwards from the sides of the shaggy head, and from the bald, horrible unnatural bony skull, which was caught by the light of the candles, four enormous curved horns spread out—sideways and up . . . The Goat turned round again after receiving the last kiss (of homage), holding between its hoofs a wooden cross about four feet in length. With a sudden violent motion it dashed the crucifix against the stone, breaking it into two pieces. Then the cat-headed man, who seemed to be acting the part of the Chief Priest, picked them up. He threw the broken end of the shaft towards a waiting group, who pounced upon it and smashed it into matchwood with silent ferocity, while he planted the crucifix end upside down in the ground before the Goat."

Terrible things which we would never dare do for they are taboo—yet we all have had, on occasion, a sneaking desire to do them (or similar)! Being adult people of course we are able to hold rein on these innermost feelings, yet there are occasional outbreaks by some people who lose control. People who allow the terrible forces within man to be unleashed. The most recent example of this was the murder of actress Sharon Tate and her friends. The words "cult death", "ritual slaying", "black mass", were much used by the popular press during the initial investigations of this case. Since California is so extraordinarily cult-conscious, and reporters are so very conscious of the newspaper-selling power of such phrases, it is not surprising that the deaths were so described.

The West Coast seems to have become the natural home of the "way out". *Esquire* magazine, in March 1970, dealt comprehensively with the wild and oftimes crazy ideas that hold sway there. Tom Burke, a reporter, had the following account from a young girl singer: "These people, man, are *dangerous* . . . This party, about eight months ago, where you were greeted at the door with a glass of their special hallucinogenic formula: acids and a pinch of strychnine. Rat poison. Makes the trip very physical. You went in and there were three altars. On two of them, these boys were tied with leather thongs. They were sobbing. These two faggots dressed as nuns—one had a goatee—were beating them with big black rosaries. On the middle altar there was a very young girl. This guy wearing a goat's head had crushed a live frog on her privates. When I came in he had just cut a little cross on her stomach; not deep but the party had just got started."

A woman who calls herself Princess Leda Amun Ra holds court in one area; Samson De Brier, a self-styled witch—of the "good", or "white", variety—in another. There is the "Arch Druid Bishop" Morloch, who leads Black Masses;

Louise Huebner, dabbling in various aspects; Lotte von Strahl, a sensitive; Frederic Adler, a would-be witch; Robin Poper, who pushes Kundalini Yoga. A motley collection of occultists and pseudo-occultists, not a few of them led more by drugs than any real knowledge of the Occult Arts. The two main ways of witchcraft can most certainly be found there—though the emphasis would seem to be on the *Rosemary's Baby*/ early Christian variety.

CHAPTER 2

STERN VOICES OF AUTHORITY

"Thou shalt not suffer a witch to live" sternly admonishes the Bible. But what did the Bible actually mean by "witch"? It has been pointed out, by the late Dr. Joseph Kaster among others, that the original word was *venefica* (meaning "poisoner") rather than *malefica* ("witch"). "Thou shalt not suffer a *poisoner* to live" then makes far better sense. Witches, as followers of the Old Religion, certainly had a great knowledge of poisons through their necessary knowledge of all herbs. But though a witch had this knowledge of poisons that did not automatically make all poisoners witches!

The word "witch" itself comes from the Anglo-Saxon *wica* (or *wicca*) meaning "a wise one". As a Wise One the early witch had to have a vast knowledge of herbs. She—or he, for witches are of both sexes—was the local doctor and veterinarian. It would not be uncommon for a child, or even an adult, in those days to suffer poisoning from eating some strange berry or the wrong variety of mushroom. To be able to combat the poison, and administer the right antidote, the wise-woman/doctor had to know the poison itself, its properties, how fast it acted, etc. This would then explain why, many hundreds of years later when the Bible was translated into English, the two words *venefica* and *malefica* were either wrongly translated or looked upon, incorrectly, as interchangeable.

In the Old Testament we find a striking example of Spiritualism when Saul, on the eve of an important battle with the Philistines, visits a medium and through her speaks with the spirit of Samuel. Montague Summers refers to the act as necromancy. This is not so, for necromancy involves conjuring *with* a dead body, to give it back life—or at least the power of speech—in order to converse with it and obtain certain secrets. The woman of Endor certainly did not have the body of Samuel available.

She apparently "saw" Samuel by what is termed *clairvoyance*: "Then said the woman, Whom shall I bring up unto thee? And he said, Bring me up Samuel. And when the woman saw Samuel, she cried with a loud voice . . . And the king said unto her, Be not afraid: for what sawest thou? And the woman said unto Saul, I saw gods ascending out of the earth. And he said unto her, What form is he of? And she said, An old man cometh up; and he is covered with a mantle. And Saul perceiveth that it was Samuel . . ."

Obviously Saul himself did not see the apparition of Samuel. It was only the woman who could "see" him, in her mind's eye. Just as a Spiritualist medium, or clairvoyant, would do.

Nowhere in the text is the word "witch" used. She is described as "a woman that hath a familiar spirit", again as a medium claims to have a spirit "Guide". The *Witch* of Endor, then, did not exist.

The term only appears in the appended heading to the chapter—"Saul seeketh to a witch"—not in the actual text. In fact we do not even know whether she was a young woman or an old one, which emphasizes the biased approach of Montague Summers who, in describing the passage, says: "In a paroxysm of rage and fear the *haggard crone* turned to him (Saul) . . ." He also refers to her dwelling as a "remote and squalid hovel", though the Bible speaks of it only as a "house".

Along with the so-called "Witch" of Endor the best-known witches are those three hags encountered by Macbeth, on the blasted heath. They would seem to be the very epitome of the species, huddled round their cauldron, chanting spells and throwing in all sorts of horrible-sounding ingredients. Yet were they really so horrible? For instance, "tongue of dog" and "adder's fork" were actually the names of plants. This is the case in a number of instances of old country cures, chants, spells and the like. The dread-sounding "sleepwort" is nothing but an old name for lettuce, believed to be a soporific. "Fox' paw" is the familiar foxglove; "Dragon's Blood" is a scarlet gum resin, and "Bird's Tongue" is the European Ash.

* * *

The first actual papal bull directly against witchcraft was that of Alexander IV, launched in

1258. He followed this with a second in 1260. Many more bulls followed, by a number of Popes, but none received the attention accorded that of Innocent VIII in 1484. This bull was especially important not for its content but for its distribution. With the coming of printing Innocent's bull was distributed far and wide, thus having much greater effect than its predecessors. It was reprinted as an introduction to the infamous *Malleus Maleficarum* (which will be dealt with fully in the next chapter).

One of the main contentions of the "New Religion" (Christianity) against the Old was that the *Wica*, or witches, worshipped and entered into a pact with Satan. This compact is nowhere mentioned in the Old Testament; it is fresh "ammunition" brought to bear on the Old Religion in the intensified attack by the New around the fourteenth/fifteenth century. The supposed pact was the means whereby witchcraft could be brought under the jurisdiction of the Inquisition, in that it made witchcraft an act of heresy. George Gifford spoke for Protestant England when he said "A witch by the word of God ought to die the death not because she killeth men . . . but because she dealeth with devils".

Up until that time Christianity had been the religion of the upper classes—the peoples of the towns and cities rather than the country people. There had been conversions taking place for years, but eventually saturation point seemed to be reached. Whole countries, such as Britain, would be partially converted then, with a new king ascending the throne, would revert back to the Old Religion. The king might, at a later date, be converted and swing the country back again to Christianity. So it went on, first one way then the other. Charlemagne had a seemingly brilliant idea to convert the Saxons. He had the bishops bless the waters of a river then, further downstream, drove the men through the river at sword-point. Many conversions were as superficial as this.

It was therefore as late as the early fourteenth century that Christianity decided to really get down to the serious business of conversion—whether the recipients wanted it or not. This was to lead, as we shall see, to the persecutions—the war-cry was to be "Convert . . . or die!"

In 1664 there was a witch trial at Bury St. Edmunds, in Suffolk County, England. The presiding justice was Sir Matthew Hale, one of England's most eminent judges. Two old widows, Rose Cullender and Amy Duny, were charged with bewitching six young girls and a baby boy. The boy had apparently been seized with fainting turns and his mother, suspecting witchcraft, consulted a wiseman-cum-doctor. He advised her to hang the child's crib blanket in the chimney corner for a day. She was then to take it down at nightfall and, should she then see something strange, to throw the object into the fire. The mother followed these instructions and, on taking down the blanket, was startled to see a large toad drop from it. Swiftly she picked it up with a pair of tongs and dropped it into the fire. There was, so we are told, a flash and a bang and the toad vanished. That same evening Amy Duny was sitting by her own fire when the flames suddenly flared up and badly scorched her. This seemed proof that the toad was actually Amy. When the baby boy later died and his mother became crippled it seemed conclusive proof that Amy was getting back at them for being burned.

The other children had severe pains and started vomiting nails and pins. When either of the two old women approached them, in the courtroom, they groaned and writhed in agony. Some of the magistrates present, however, felt that this behaviour, on the part of the children, was a pretence. By blindfolding the girls and having different people touch them they were able to prove that this was so. But Sir Matthew Hale was not impressed. He rebuked the magistrates and declared that the reality of witchcraft was not open to question since it was especially mentioned in the Bible. The jury reached a verdict of guilty in less than half an hour, and two weeks later the two old women were hung—protesting their innocence to their last breath.

Robin Goodfellow—the God of the Old Religion.

Sir Matthew Hale, speaking of the case, said, "That there were such Creatures as *Witches* he had no doubt at all; For *First* the Scriptures had affirmed so much. *Secondly,* The wisdom of all Nations had provided Laws against such Persons, which is an Argument of their confidence of such a Crime. And such hath been the judgement of this Kingdom, as appears by that Act of Parliament which hath provided Punishments proportionable to the quality of the Offence. And desired them (the jury), strictly to observe their Evidence; and desired the great God of Heaven to direct their Hearts in this weighty thing they had in hand: For to Condemn the Innocent, and to let the Guilty go free, were both an abomination to the Lord." So convinced a believer in witchcraft was Hale that, despite conflicting evidence and protestations from the "gentlemen of the court" he found the defendants guilty and hung them. "It was a trial much considered by the judges of New England", wrote Cotton Mather.

The Reverend Cotton Mather was one of the leading lights against witchcraft in America. Although this country entered into the witchcraft scene much later than Europe Mather's comments, and acts, are very pertinent to the feelings of the Church in Europe at the earlier stage. Cotton was the son of Increase Mather, who was president of Harvard, pastor of the Second Church, and ambassador-extraordinary from Massachusetts to

Cotton Mather—1662-1728.

England. Cotton Mather himself entered Harvard at the age of twelve. At twenty-five he had charge of Boston's North Church, the largest in New England.

In 1689 Cotton Mather published a book called *Memorable Providences Relating to Witchcraft and Possessions*. It was extremely well received and had a wide circulation. Included in the book were Mather's findings on the case of the Goodwin children, of Boston, and Witch Glover. In a case similar to that of Salem, but predating it, four children of a religious family had suffered fits supposedly caused by an old Irish washerwoman. Although the woman, Goody Glover, was hung the fits continued. Mather visited Goody Glover in her cell, prior to sentence being carried out. Although she wanted no part of him he insisted on praying for her there. He says that she was utterly unpenitent, and confessed to him that she had made a covenant with Satan and that she had been in the habit of going to meetings at which Satan was present.

Mather took one of the children, a girl named Martha, into his house to study her and try to effect a cure. John Fiske described what developed (in *New France and New England*, 1902): "The girl showed herself an actress of elf-like precocity and shrewdness. She wished to prove that she was bewitched, and she seems to have known Mather's prejudices against Quakers, Papists, and the

Church of England; for she could read Quaker books and Catholic books fluently, and seemed quite in love with the Book of Common Prayer, but she could not read a word in the Bible or any book of Puritan theology, and even in her favorite Prayer Book, whenever she came to the Lord's Prayer she faltered and failed. Gradually the young minister's firm good sense and kindness prevailed in calming her and making her discard such nonsense, but during the cure her symptoms showed the actress."

Mather wrote that "she went on Fantastick Journeys to the witches' Rendezvouse." Actually she sat astride a chair and rocked backwards and forwards as though riding a horse. In his later book, *Wonders of the Invisible World*, Mather wrote "In these Hellish Meetings these Monsters have associated themselves to do no less a Thing than, To destroy the Kingdom of Jesus Christ, in these parts of the World. The Witches say, that they form themselves much after the manner of Congregational Churches."

Montague Summers, on no evidence whatsoever, says "There can be no doubt that at Salem (See Chapter 6) the traditional rites of the hideous black worship were precisely observed, allowing, of course, that it was a Protestant Communion and not the Holy Mass that was the model of their hellish liturgy. These practises must have been carefully handed down and taught to the

New England representatives of the witch society."

Another of the respected writers and "authorities" on witchcraft, in the seventeenth century, Joseph Glanvill, who wrote *Saducismus Triumphatus* (subtitled, "full and plain evidence concerning witches and apparitions"), described as "perhaps the ablest book published which defends, after analysis and with detailed evidence, the belief in witches". Glanvill was a Chaplain to King Charles II. He wrote, "A Witch is one who can do. or seems to do strange things, beyond the known Power of Art and ordinary Nature, by virtue of a Confederacy with Evil Spirits . . . The strange things are really performed, and are not all Impostures and Delusions. The Witch occasions, but is not the Principle Efficient, she seems to do it, but the Spirit performs the wonder, sometimes immediately, as in Transportations and Possessions, sometimes by applying other Natural Causes, as in raising Storms, and inflicting Diseases, sometimes using the Witch as an Instrument, and either by the Eyes or Touch, conveying Malign Influences: And these things are done by virtue of a Covenant, or Compact betwixt the Witch and an Evil Spirit. A Spirit, viz. an Intelligent Creature of the Invisible World, whether one of the Evil Angels called *Devils*, or an Inferior *Daemon* or *Spirit*, or a wicked Soul departed; but one that is able and ready for mischief, and whether altogether Incorporeal or not, appertains not to this Question."

In France in 1670 a dozen women were condemned to be burned at the stake (the penalty there, and in Scotland, unlike England and New England where witches were hung) for witchcraft. There was an appeal to the king, Louis XIV, and he spared their lives on condition that they should leave the country. There was great astonishment, and not a little indignation, at this clemency. So much so that the parliament of Normandy saw fit to send a petition to the king. It said, "Your parliament have thought it their duty on occasion of these crimes, the greatest that man can commit, to make you acquainted with the general and uniform feeling of the people of this province with regard to them; it being moreover a question in which are concerned the glory of God and the relief of your suffering subjects, who groan under their fears from the threats and menaces of this sort of persons . . . We humbly supplicate your Majesty to reflect once more upon the extraordinary results which proceed from the malevolence of these people; on the loss of goods and chattels, and the deaths from unknown diseases, which are often the consequence of their menaces, . . . all of which may easily be proved to your Majesty's satisfaction by the records of various trials before your parliaments."

Fiske goes on to say, "It is pleasant to be able to add that Louis XIV was too well versed in the professional etiquette of royalty to withdraw a pardon which he had once granted, and so the poor women were saved from the flames. What we have especially to note is that the highest court of Normandy, representing the best legal knowledge of that province, in defining witchcraft as the infliction of disease or the destruction of property by unknown and mysterious means, describes it as the greatest of all crimes . . ."

In Protestant Britain the official "guide" for the witch persecutors was *Demonologie*, written by King James the First, in 1597. In James' first parliamentary Bill he introduced legislation that made witchcraft punishable by death. This was the most severe enactment ever in Britain and was far harsher than the previous legislation against witchcraft enacted by Queen Elizabeth I. The witches' supposed pacts with the Devil were very much emphasized, in Britain, from this time on.

As Rossell Robbins points out, in his heavily editorialized *Encyclpaedia of Witchcraft and Demonology*, "The King's bias influenced the translation of the Bible; whenever the Septuagint had 'one that consulteth pythonic spirits', the Authorized Version (1603) used James' definition of a witch in his *Daemonologie*, 'a consulter with familiar spirits'. The Bible was thus angled to justify conceptions completely unknown to it."

James certainly had great credulity of the supposed traditions of witchcraft. He believed that witches could be transported through the air "by the force of the spirit which is their conductor." He did not, however, believe that they could be transformed into a "little beast or foule" and pass through "whatsoever house or Church, though all ordinarie passages be closed". In his speech at the Tolbooth, in 1591, he said ". . . witchcraft, which is a thing grown very common amongst us, I know it to be the most abominable sin . . . by God's law punishable by death . . . I call them witches which do renounce God and yield themselves wholly to the Devil . . ."

CHAPTER 3
ACTIONS SPEAK LOUDER THAN WORDS

I have mentioned the publication of the *Malleus Maleficarum* in 1486. It is described by Rossell Robbins as "without question the most important and sinister work on demonology ever written." Pennethorne Hughes speaks of it as "a most hideous document. It defied all that we mean by the laws of evidence. It presumed guilt and it advocated torture." It is certainly a terrifying testimony to the ways of the Church at that time. It details all the many tricks and tortures that were felt justified to obtain a confession, presuming that all charged withwitchcraft were necessarily guilty. The book is in three parts, the first of which treats "the three necessary concomitants of witchcraft which are the Devil, a Witch, and the permission of Almighty God." Here the reader is first admonished that to *not* believe in witchcraft is heresy. Points are then covered on whether children can be generated by Incubi and Succubi; witches' copulation with the Devil; whether witches can sway the minds of men to love or hatred; whether witches can hebetate the powers of generation or obstruct the venereal act; whether witches may work some prestidigitatory illusion so that the male organ appears to be entirely removed and separate from the body; various ways (that the witches may) kill the child conceived in the womb." etc., etc..

The second part, "Treating of the methods by which the works of witchcraft are wrought and directed, and how they may be successfully annulled and dissolved," deals with "the several methods by which Devils through witches entice and allure the innocent to the increase of that horrid craft and company; the way whereby a formal pact with evil is made; how they transport from place to place; how witches impede and prevent the power of procreation; how as it were they deprive man of his virile member; how witch midwives commit most horrid crimes when they either kill children or offer them to devils in most accursed wise; how witches—injure cattle, raise and stir up hailstorms and tempests and cause lightning to blast both men and beasts." Then follow remedies for all the above.

The third part of the book "Relating to the judicial proceedings in both the ecclesiastical and civil courts against witches and indeed all heretics", is perhaps the most important. It is here that the order of the trial is dealt with. "Who are the fit and proper judges for the trial of witches?" is the first question. It goes on to "The method of initiating a process; the solemn adjuration and re-examination of witnesses; the quality and condition of witnesss; whether mortal enemies may be admitted as witnesses." Here we are told that "the testimony of men of low repute and criminals, and of servants against their masters, is admitted. . ... it is to be noted that a witness is not necessarily to be disqualified because of every

The Swimming of a Witch—1612.

sort of enmity." We learn that, in the case of witchcraft, virtually anybody may give evidence, though in any other case they would not be admitted. Even the evidence of young children was admissable.

This third part goes on with "how the trial is to be proceeded with and continued, whether the witch is to be imprisoned; what is to be done after the arrest; points to be observed by the Judge before the formal examination in the place of detention and torture; how she must be questioned; the continuing of the torture; how they are to be shaved in those parts where they use to conceal the Devil's masks and tokens; various means of overcoming their obstinacy in keeping silence and refusal to confess; the trial by red-hot iron; the manner of pronouncing sentence," etc., etc.

It is obvious, from the above, that the authors of the *Malleus Maleficarum* had certain obsessions. A large number of the chapters are, for example, concerned with sexual aspects of witchcraft. But, as Julio Baroja points out, it was not the theologians and scholastic philosophers who were responsible for putting these obsessions into practise. It was the law and lawyers, Catholic *and* Protestant, who made the greatest use of it, from its first appearance right through to the early eighteenth century.

Who were the authors of this infamous work? They were two Dominicans named Jakob Sprenger and Heinrich (Institor) Kramer, who were the Chief Inquisitors for Germany. To give an idea of the sort of men they were there is a story—well authenticated—that Kramer was once witch-hunting in the Tyrol. To achieve his ends he bribed an old woman to climb into a baker's oven and scream that the Devil had put her there. Then, from inside the oven, she was to name some of the Devil's followers in the area. This the woman did and Kramer played his game through to the bitter end. Seizing the women named by his confederate he put them to the most cruel of tortures in order to extract a "confession" from them. Obviously obsessed the two authors would go to any lengths to have the witches burned.

The late Dr. Gerald Gardner, one of the foremost authorities on witchcraft, was one of the first to point out a forgery perpetrated by Sprenger and Kramer. At the time of publication of the *Malleus Maleficarum* the appointed Censor of books was the University of Cologne. When Kramer and Sprenger presented their work all but four of the professors wanted nothing to do with it. As Gardner says, "nothing daunted this precious pair of scoundrels proceeded to forge a document which purported to show the approbation of the whole Faculty." Even the four professors who had not rejected it entirely had limited their comments to the facts that there was nothing in the first two parts that was averse to Catholic teaching, and that the third part was true because of the character of the various witnesses quoted there.

Joseph Hansen, the learned archivist of Cologne, actually exposed the forgery in 1898. Apparently copies of the book actually sold in Cologne did not carry the Approbation, but it was in those to be circulated elsewhere. At Sprenger's death, in 1495, although he was a member of the Theological Faculty he was not given the traditional Requiem Mass by the University.

The appearance of the *Malleus Maleficarum* was in effect, the signal for the persecutions to begin in earnest. As Robbins says, it "opened the floodgates of the inquisitional hysteria." Up until that time the Church had tried, half-heartedly, to stamp out the remains of the Old Religion. Where beliefs and practises were too deeply engrained they had been incorporated into the New Religion. Many of the first Christian churches were purposely built on the sites of old pagan temples or meeting places. The bishops knew that the populace came to these particular spots to worship, and had done so for hundreds if not thousands of years. So why not cash-in on the habit?

There were other more definite adoptions from the Old Religions, especially in the early formative years of Christianity. The idea of the Trinity, for instance, was taken from the old Egyptian triad. Osiris, Isis and Horus became God, Mary and Jesus. December 25th, as the birth-date of Jesus, was borrowed from Mithraism—which also believed in a second coming and indulged in the "Eating of God." In many religions of the ancient world were found immaculate conceptions and sacrifice of the god for the salvation of the people.

However, as Christianity gained in strength so it was able to push back its rival religions. It has frequently been said that the gods of an old religion become known as "devils" to the new religion. This was very much the case with the gods of the Wica. The practises of the pagans (remembering that there was originally no evil connotation to the word "pagan". It comes from the latin *pagani* and means simply "one who dwells in the country".) were twisted, misrepresented, to give them an air of evil. Fertility beliefs stayed long in the hearts of the country people. Although famers no longer think of the moon as symbolizing a Goddess of Fertility yet, even today, do they still sow and reap according to the phases of the moon.

So from time to time the Church issued edicts against one or another pagan practise or belief. As late as the end of the thirteenth century a priest, at Inverkeithing, Scotland, was reprimanded for leading his parishioners in a fertility dance through the churchyard. Two years earlier, in 1280, the Abbot of Whalley was excommunicated for employing a "wise man" to "discover the body of his brother, drowned in the (River) Ouse." In 1343 the Bishop of Coventry was accused of worshipping the old God of Nature—labelled by his accusers "the Devil".

It was realised by the Church, then, that just to convert was not enough. Conversions, even nominal ones, had been all very well up until this time but now it was to be a case of "if they will not convert, then they must die!" Every sign of the Old Religion was to be stamped out. Every member of the Wica was to be made to confess his beliefs—or the beliefs attributed to him by the Christians—and then be punished for them. The book of rules—the *Malleus Maleficarum*—had appeared; it was time to act. Since witchcraft was most prevalent amongst the peasant classes it was to be the easiest thing to discover and punish. The local priests were forced, by their superiors, to take harsh action against what they had previously viewed with leniency.

With this sudden onslaught, which soon rose to outright hysteria, no one felt safe. First ordinary people, later many in high places, felt the fury of the Church. Everywhere was suspicion and fear. Although the Renaissance brought a greater latitude of mind and belief it held no tolerance for witchcraft. The Reformers in fact seemed more incensed than had the Catholics. Luther himself said "I have no compassion on the witches. I would burn them all."

In England witches were still regarded as criminals rather than heretics—hence they were hung rather than burned at the stake. But one problem was that no one knew for sure exactly who the witches were. Your neighbor might be one, or your best friend. The only safe course seemed to be to accuse someone else before they accused you! Of course this also provided many golden opportunities for the unscrupulous. If a man wanted to buy his neighbor's land but the price was too high he had only to accuse his neighbor of witchcraft and he would be hauled away leaving his land to be sold for what it would fetch. Children—whose evidence was acceptable on the authority of the *Malleus Maleficarum*—would accuse old ladies who had chased them out of their apple orchards. Business rivals would dispose of one another. Farmers who had a bad harvest would accuse an old woman of bewitching them. If a child fell ill its mother would look to the neighbors for the cause.

The prisons filled up and the courts worked overtime. A person might lay in his cell for years awaiting trial. Then, even if found not guilty, he could not leave until he had paid the bill presented by the jailer for his keep.

Once accused of witchcraft a confession was looked for. There were ways to obtain this, the most obvious being torture. It has been said that torture was not employed in England but this is not really so. It may not have been officially employed, nor as frequently as elsewhere, but there are certainly many records of its use. It certainly was against English law to employ torture but then there were many things that could be done to the witches which the authorities did not consider such. Keeping the accused from sleeping, for instance, or making them walk continuously hour after hour. One favorite was to tie the accused cross-legged to a stool and keep him there without food for several days and nights.

There was one man, in Suffolk County, England, who came in contact with a witch. He realised, in turning her over to the authorities, that there was a worthwhile business to be made from witch-finding. The man's name was Matthew Hopkins. He was an unsuccessful lawyer and the son of a minister, James Hopkins. Witch-finders flourished, especially in Scotland, at this time. Hopkins had read James I's *Daemonologie*, Richard Bernard's *Advice to Grand Jurymen*, and an account of the Lancashire Witches of 1612. This was his only training as a witch-finder. The first witch he had found was an old woman, with only one leg, named Elisabeth Clarke. She was tortured by enforced sleeplessness for three days and nights before she would "confess" to Hopkins. Among the things to which she admitted were that she had certain "imps" who would do her bidding. The names of these were Ilemauzar, Pyewackett, Griezzell Greedigutt, Vinegar Tom, Sacke and Sugar, Jarmara, Newes and Pecke in the Crowne. Hopkins testified in court that he had personally seen these imps.

With the confession of Elisabeth Clarke another five women were arrested who, in turn, accused others. Hopkins had by now enlisted the help of two assistants, John Stearne, a Puritan like Hopkins, and a woman named Goody Phillips. By the time this trio had passed on to other parts of Suffolk—and thence to Norfolk, Cambridgeshire, Huntingdonshire and Bedfordshire—a total of twenty-nine people had been charged.

As an example of the evidence on which they were brought to trial, one woman was charged with being a witch simply because a young hare was seen to sit in the road in front of her house.

Hopkins' method of working was to visit a town and go straightaway to the Town Hall. There he would advise the authorities that he was in possession of the Devil's own list of witches in that area. He assumed the title "Witch-Finder" (and in at least one instance, "Witch-Finder General") and charged a fee of twenty shillings, plus expenses, for every witch brought to trial and convicted. He and his companions would take into custody anyone suspected, however vaguely, of witchcraft and proceed to test them.

There were various ways of testing. The first was to search for the Devil's Mark. This was supposedly an insensitive spot somewhere on the body. The trio would strip their victim then keep plunging needles into her. Some later witch-finders would ensure "finding" this spot by using false needles—bodkins whose points would slide into the handles so that, to an observer, the blade had been plunged right in, yet the victim could feel nothing.

A true witch was also supposed to possess a supernumerary nipple; a spot—quite distinct from the Devil's Mark—where she would feed her imp, or Domestic Familiar. This was invariably a small creature like a rat, a mole or a toad. It would suck a drop of blood from its owner, in that way becoming an extension of its owner. It was a creature with magical powers and was sometimes passed on from mother to daughter. Although there had been mention of such familiars previously it was due to Matthew Hopkins that emphasis was placed on them and they became, for no good reason, inextricably linked with the witch in the popular mind.

It would be unusual to find anyone who did not have some blemish, mole, freckle, excrescence of some sort that could not be taken for this supernumerary nipple. Hopkins' female assistant, Goody Phillips, frequently seemed to find them in the "secretest parts".

Yet another test for witchcraft was the swimming test. For this the victim would have the thumb of her right hand tied to the big toe of her left foot, and the left thumb tied to the toe of her right foot. In this crouched position she would be tossed into the water of a pond, river, or stream. The belief was that the water, being a symbol of admission to the Christian Church, would not receive a witch. So if a woman floated she was obviously guilty. If she was received, and sank, then she was innocent and, if she was lucky, she would be hauled out before she drowned. Invariably, because of the air contained in their voluminous clothes, the women floated and were found guilty.

King James had written that "God hath appointed (for a supernaturall signe of the monstrous impietie of Witches) that the water shall refuse to receiue them to her bosome, that haue shaken off them the sacred Water of Baptisme, and wilfully refused the benefite thereof." However William Perkins an eminent theologian, in 1608 pointed out "To iustifie the casting of a Witch into the water, it is alledged, that hauing made a couenant with the deuill, shee hath renounced her Baptisme, and hereupon there growes an Antipathie between her, and water. *Ans.* This allegation serues to no purpose: for all water is not the water of Baptisme, but that onely which is vsed in the very act of Baptisme, and not before or after. The element out of the vse of the Sacrament, is no Sacrament, but returnes again to its common vse." All of which mattered not a jot to Hopkins who carried on dunking old women left, right and center.

Hopkins, carried away with his successes and thinking of himself as a benefactor to Christendom, did not hesitate to accuse John Lowes, pastor of Brandeston, of witchcraft. Lowes had been pastor for over fifty years. He had, at eighty, grown into a crotchety old man and did not get on well with his parishioners. They, for their part, seized the opportunity to destroy him. Hopkins and his assistants kept the parson awake for several days and nights, walking him up and down, until he was utterly exhausted and did not know what he was saying or doing. In this way did Hopkins secure from him a detailed confession to having sunk a boatful of sailors at Ipswich.

By 1646 Hopkins' influence was on the decline and he retired from the "business". According to James Howell (*Familiar Letters*, 1648) in the two counties of Essex and Sussex alone nearly three hundred supposed witches had been arraigned through Hopkins, and almost all of these had been executed.

From the *Malleus Maleficarum* it was shown that the best way to prove witchcraft, and especially the pact with the Devil, was through confession by the witch herself. To obtain that confession it was frequently necessary to resort to torture. This was not so much to obtain *a* confession, but to obtain *the particular* confession — the specified answers to the listed questions.

Robbins points out that burning at the stake, as the ultimate punishment, was supported by the Italian Professor Bartolo, in 1350, when he applied to witches the words of Christ, "If a man abide not in me (i.e. the Catholic Church), he is cast forth as a branch . . . and men gather them and cast them into the fire and they are burned."

Many of the tortures employed are illustrated in engravings of the times. One such engraving shows thirty people imprisoned in a small room, chained together in pairs. Deprived of food they eventually became delirious through hunger and began tearing each other to pieces. Other illustrations show people stripped naked and being dragged along a tightly-drawn rope which, acting like a saw, cut the body in two. Some were tied to stakes and had fires lit a short distance away, so that they would burn very, very slowly. There was also disembowelling, eye-gouging and flogging.

One common form of torture was the *strappado* (from the latin *strappare*, to pull), a way of pulling the arms from their sockets. It was done by tying the victim's hands behind his back then passing the rope over a pulley in the ceiling. The torturors would haul on the rope, lifting the victim off the ground. They would then tie weights to the feet until his arms came out of their sockets at the shoulders. Occasionally, to vary the pace, the victim would be hauled up into the air close to the ceiling then allowed to drop, but stopping short of the ground. In the case of a woman who was pregnant it was considered great sport to actually drop her on her belly.

The thumbscrews were frequently employed, as were leg-vises (often called "Spanish Boots" because of their use in the Spanish Inquisition). The thumbscrews were, basically, small vises designed to crush not only the thumbs but also fingers and toes. The boots were of two types. One type was adjustable, again as a vise, so that they could be tightened up on the legs until the bones were crushed. The other type were over-large metal boots. The feet would be placed in them and then boiling water or oil would be poured in.

The laws of England (and of New England) were, on the whole, honorably free from this particular form of barbarity. There was, however, one form of procedure which did involve torture.

This was known as *peine forte et dure*. If a prisoner refused to plead, and to state the required desire to be tried "by God and my country", then he could be made to undergo the "pressing". He would be laid on his back on a stone floor and then iron weights, or heavy rocks, would be piled on top of him until he either pleaded or (as in the case of Giles Cory, at Salem, Massachusetts) he died.

CHAPTER 4

POLITICAL WITCHCRAFT?

"Witchcraft was inextricably mixed with politics", says Montague Summers in his introduction to his translation of the *Malleus Maleficarum*. He cites various instances: the Earl of Kent was accused, in 1232, by the Bishop of Winchester, of having won the favor of Henry III through "charms and incantations"; the Duchess of Gloucester, in 1441, was charged with trying to bring about the death of Henry VI through the agencies of "a most notorious evoker of demons"; Edward III's mistress, Alice Perrers, secured the monarch's affections through the use of spells.

In 1590 there was a conspiracy against James VI of Scotland (who became James I of England). It was led by Francis, Earl of Bothwell, who was a claimant to the throne should the king die without an heir. Bothwell was the leader, or Grand Master, of a coven of witches in North Berwick. These witches worked magic against the king, at one time causing a storm in the North Sea when he and his queen were sailing across to Scotland from Denmark. Another time they made a wax figure of James and tormented it.

The conspiracy against James first came to light through the actions of a serving-maid named Geillis Duncan. Geillis was rapidly acquiring a reputation for curing the sick, through occult means, when her employer started to investigate her. He was David Seaton, deputy-bailiff of a small town called Tranent, near Edinburgh. He decided in his own mind, that Geillis' skill was a gift from the Devil. Taking the law into his own hands he set about interrogating her using a thumb-screw, and other implements, in the process. He finally got her to "confess" that she was indeed involved with the Devil.

On Geillis finally being turned over to the authorities she started to implicate others and inferred that they had all been working together in a plot against the king. One of the people she implicated was a Dr. John Fian, a schoolmaster, of Lothian. Fian was apparently the secretary, or recorder, of the witch group. A copy of *News From Scotland*, published in 1591, carries a picture of him sitting at a desk alongside a group of witches.

There are many stories told about John Fian but the most amusing is the story of the cow. It is said that he had fallen in love with the elder sister of one of his young pupils. He asked the pupil to bring him a lock of the girl's hair, intending to work a charm through it. When the boy brought him the hair he worked a charm that would make its owner fall in love with him. The girl, however, apparently suspected Fian for he found himself being followed everywhere by a big, brown cow. The hair he had been given had come not from the girl but, from the tail of the cow!

John Fian was tortured until he confessed and signed this confession in King James' presence. At some time, either in his interrogation or in the actual signed confession (which was later lost or stolen), he implicated the Earl of Bothwell. After his torture he was returned to his cell and, surprisingly managed to escape. It is not unlikely that he realised what he had done, in implicating Bothwell, and was desperate to warn the Earl.

At any rate Fian was finally recaptured. On his re-examination he flatly denied all that he had originally confessed and then fell silent. Despite firther torture he would sav nothing and went mutely to his execution.

Also named by Geillis Duncan was a woman. Agnes Sampson, of Haddington. Agnes was questioned and also searched for the "Devil's Mark" (She was shaved all over and finally her examiners claimed to have found what they were looking for in the pudenda). When tortured Agnes Sampson told some amazing stories. She told how some two hundred witches had gathered together in a churchyard in North Berwick. They had got there by sailing along in seives, drinking wine as they went. At the churchyard there was singing and dancing, with Geillis Duncas playing the tunes on a Jew's-harp, or "trump". At this point the king had Geillis play him a dance on the instrument and, apparently, thoroughly enjoyed it.

Inside the church, at North Berwick, the Devil

himself (or his earthly representative), appeared to the witches and preached to them. He then had them give him the *oscullum infami* before departing: "Now efter that the deuell had endit his admonitions, he cam down out of the pulpit, and caused all the company to com and kiss his ers, quhilk (which) they said was cauld lyk yce."

King James was not overly impressed with Agnes Sampson's stories and actually called her a liar. However he was suddenly stunned, according to his own report, when Agnes went on to tell him exactly what his Queen had said to him on the first night of their marriage, when they were in Oslo, Norway.

Since this was something she could not know by normal means he had to believe there was also truth in the rest of the stories she had told. One of these had concerned a spell for his downfall. It involved the gathering of venom from a toad and subsequently spreading it on some item of the king's clothing. In this way to bewitch him.

When the king had gone to Denmark to marry his fifteen-year-old Queen, Anne, his ship had been badly tossed about in an unnatural storm. From Agnes Sampson James now learned that this storm had been caused by the witches. They had taken a cat and christened it. Then to each paw they had fastened a human limb—taken from a grave—and had tossed the cat into the sea. This caused the storm.

Another magical charm against the king had been the making of a waxen image, or "picture." This had been prepared by Agnes and some others, then carefully wrapped in a linen cloth and taken to one of the meetings with the Devil, who inspected it closely. Being satisfied he had the witches pass it around, each saying over it: "This is King James the Sixth, ordained to be consumed at the instance of a nobleman, Francis Earl Bothwell!" At one of the subsequent meetings an old ploughman called Grey Mill happened to remark "Nothing ails the king yet, God be thanked" and, according to Melville (*Memoirs*), "the deuell gaif him a gret blaw!"

It is almost certain that the nobleman who played the part of the Devil at the witch-meetings, always wearing a masked disguise, was in fact Francis of Bothwell himself. Barbara Napier, one of the accused witches, described him: "The Devil start up in the pulpit, like a mickle black man, with a black beard sticking out like a goat's beard; and a high ribbed nose, falling down sharp like the beak of a hawk; with a long rumpill (tail)."

In all over sixty people were implicated in the North Berwick case. Among them Barbara Napier, sister-in-law to the Laird of Carschoggill, and Dame Euphemia McCalyan, daughter of Lord Cliftonhall. Dame McCalyan was burned alive at the stake, while Barbara Napier—through claiming to be pregnant—was eventually freed.

The Earl of Bothwell himself, although he denied any connection with the witches, was put into Edinburgh Castle but later managed to escape. He left Scotland and fled to Italy, settling in Naples. It seems that he really did believe in himself as the representative of the Devil and his evil powers, for he wrote to a friend "You Christians are deceitful and headstrong. If you have a powerful desire, you abandon your Master and seek my aid. And when your objective is gained, you spurn me as a foe and return to your deity ... Yet, if you commit yourself to me in written and autographed form ... I shall give you what you desire."

Two years later James pardoned Bothwell but the Earl, perhaps wisely, stayed in Italy. He eventually died there, it is said penilessly.

Witches bringing a Shower of Rain.
Ulrich Molitor, De Lamiis et phitonicis mulieribus
(Constance, 1489)

CHAPTER 5

OLD ENGLAND...

Witchcraft in England really started several thousand years ago, as will be seen from Chapter Seven. But for the purposes of looking at the ways of witchcraft from the Church's point of view it did not really start—or become a problem—until the beginning of the sixteenth century.

The first Tudor Act against witchcraft was passed in 1542. It was aimed not at the devil-worship type of witchcraft so prominent in later years but at sorcery, "wasting, consuming, or destroying any person in body, members or goods or to provoke any person to unlawfully use." It was against incantations and treasure-seeking; it was actually against *magic* and its use, rather than against witchcraft *per se*. There was no mention of the Devil and his worship, nor of covens, nor Sabbat assemblies. In 1563, under pressure from the Church, Queen Elizabeth I finally introduced an Act against witchcraft that brought the doings of the Devil into it, and gave the death penalty for involving him. The first major trial under this new law was that of the Chelmsford Witches.

There were three defendants, Agnes Waterhouse, her daughter Joan Waterhouse and Elizabeth Francis. At the first examination the Reverend Thomas Cole, of Stamford Rivers, and Sir John Fortescue, later Chancellor of the Exchequer, were present. At the second hearing they were replaced by John Southcote, justice of the

Queen's bench, and Sir Gilbert Gerard, the queen's attorney.

When Elizabeth Francis was examined she seemed only too happy to admit to various charges of villainy. She told how her grandmother had given her a white spotted cat, when she was a child, named Satan. If she fed him and looked after him, she said, then Satan gave her whatever she wanted—or almost. For example, Elizabeth decided that the wealthy Andrew Byles would make an ideal husband for her. She said so to her cat, who—"in a strange hollow voice" —promised her that she should have him. Although, apparently, Andrew Byles got Elizabeth to bed a number of times he did not stay and marry her. Understandably chagrined she then willed Satan to "touch his body, which he forthwith did, whereof he died". She then found that she was pregnant, but once again the cat came to her aid. He told her of a certain herb which she took and consequently miscarried.

Later Satan did provide her with a husband, though not as rich a one as the late Andrew Byles. The marriage was not a happy one, however, and Elizabeth—never satisfied it seems—called upon the cat to lame her husband, Christopher Francis, and kill the child she had recently borne him. Again Satan obliged.

In all Elizabeth Francis kept her obliging pet for fifteen years. She had been instructed by her grandmother to feed it a drop of her blood whenever she asked it to do something for her. This she had done. She was able to show the court the many little red spots where she had pricked herself that the cat might suck the blood. The spots, it seemed, had never disappeared. Eventually Elizabeth gave the cat to her sister, Agnes Waterhouse, in exchange for a cake.

When Agnes was examined she claimed that she had actually changed the cat into a toad. She had done this by willing it and by saying "her Pater noster in laten" and praying "in the name of the father and of the sonne, and of the holy ghost that it wold turne into a tode". She used it to kill cattle, geese and hogs belonging to her neighbors. She then went on to bigger and better things—she killed her husband and a neighbor.

When Agnes' daughter Joan, aged eighteen, was questioned she confirmed that her mother did indeed have a toad familiar. In fact, she said, she had made use of its services herself. One day she had asked a neighbor's child for a piece of bread and cheese but had been refused. She went straight to the toad, Satan, for help. Satan said he would help her—if she would surrender to him her soul. She agreed. The toad then went off and haunted the neighbor's child in the form of a dog with horns. When the child, Agnes Brown, was called to testify she said she certainly had been so haunted. "She said that at such a day, naming the day certain, she was churning of butter and there came to her a thing like a black Dog with a face like an ape, a short tail, a chain and a silver whistle about its neck, and a pair of horns on his head, and brought in his mouth the key of the milkhouse door, and then my lord, she said, I was afraid, for he skipped and leaped to and fro, and sat on the top of a nettle." Agnes Brown was twelve years old.

Agnes Waterhouse was asked when she let the familiar suck her blood. She replied that she did not, but the jailer removed her head covering and revealed a number of red spots. She was then questioned on her church attendance and claimed to go regularly, saying that she "prayed right hartely there". She did admit, however, that Satan would not let her pray in English so she had to do it in Latin.

After a further day of questioning the jury retired and shortly returned with their verdict— Guilty. On July 29, 1566, Agnes Waterhouse was hanged. Joan Waterhouse, whose only charge was that of bewitching Agnes Brown, was found Not Guilty. Elizabeth Francis got off with one year in prison.

* * *

From this first, relatively simple, case of witchcraft it is interesting to look at a later, more complicated case. Sabbat orgies seemed to play a big part in witchcraft on the continent but were virtually absent from the English scene. One of the few sabbatical feasts of which there is record was that held at Malking Tower by the Lancashire Witches.

In 1612 opened the trial of twenty alleged witches in the county of Lancashire. It was the largest such trial to that date. The two leading figures were typical of the witch conception (or misconception) that so many people have today, of the old, withered, hag. There was Elisabeth Southerns, known as Old Demdike, who had been practising witchcraft for over forty of her eighty years. And there was her neighbor Ann Whittle, known as Old Chattox, who was also in her eighties. Old Demdike was facially deformed, with one eye higher than the other, "the one looking down, and the other looking up." Old Chattox was a wool-carder, "a very old, withered, spent and decreped creature".

Both families, who lived in the forest of Pendle in eastern Lancashire, claimed supernatural powers. Old Chattox in fact worked an early "protection racket" by promising *not* to cause harm to families in return for a yearly payment of "one aghen-dole of meale."

Although neighbors the two families of Demdike and Chattox were forever feuding. Old Demdike had a daughter, Anne Redfearn. Some years before the trial there had been a big dispute when

Elisabeth Device, discovering various clothes, food and an amount of money missing, discovered some of it in Anne Redfearn's possession.

The families came into contact with the law when young Alison Device, Elisabeth's daughter, was accused of laming a pedlar named John Law. The pedlar had apparently refused to sell her some pins. She had therefore caused her familiar to appear to him in the form of a black dog, and to lame him. From the description given in Thomas Potts' voluminous record of the trial it sounds as though the pedlar actually suffered a stroke and connected it, in his mind, with Alison Device.

Under questioning Alison implicated her mother, Elisabeth, and her grandmother, Old Demdike. She told how her grandmother had bewitched, to death, the child of a Richard Baldwin. She also told how Old Chattox and her daughter Ann had worked against Robert Nutter, of Greenhead, causing his cow to die. Robert Nutter had, apparently, tried to seduce Ann Redfearn. When she repelled him he said that he would have her evicted, for the Nutter family owned the property on which she lived. After killing Nutter's cow Ann and her mother started work on Robert himself. Others joined them in the work—the Nutters did not seem overly popular. Even Elisabeth Device worked on it, making a wax image. Within three months Robert Nutter died.

Old Demdike, Old Chattox, Ann Redfearn and Alison Device were locked-up in Lancaster castle. Elisabeth Device was not immediately arrested. She made good her freedom by calling together all the witches of the area (Pendle Forest) to meet at her mother's house, known as Malking Tower. It was on Good Friday that they met. She asked that they all assist in getting the four women out of the castle. The meeting was attended by eighteen women and four men. They brought with them food (including a sheep stolen by James Device) and drink, and a cheerful feast ensued before they got down to business.

In the business discussion it was suggested that they attempt to blow up Lancaster castle and kill the jailer. No definite plans were finally forthcoming, however, and so they concluded their meeting by naming the familiar spirit of one of those present and promising help to one Jennet Preston, who wished to murder a certain Thomas Lister (This Thomas Lister did in fact die. Before doing so he accused Jennet Preston and she was finally hanged).

Justice Nowell heard rumors of the meeting and it was not long before another nine witches were in the castle jail. Before the main trial started Old Demdike died in the prison. Old Chattox, amid tears, admitted to all of which she was charged, but the others claimed innocence. From a final total of twenty accused ten were eventually hanged. Two were sentenced to one year in jail, with periodic appearances in the pillory, and the rest were acquitted.

The highlight of the trial of the Lancashire Witches was the evidence of young Jennet Device, then nine years old. She claimed to have been witness to everything that had happened, including the meeting at Malking Tower. She had always known her mother was a witch and had many times seen her speaking with her familiar, a brown dog named Ball. Elisabeth and Ball had together killed a neighbor, John Robinson. Later they also killed his brother James and a man named Humphrey Mitton.

As young Jennet started her evidence her mother, Elisabeth, caused such a commotion that she had to be removed from the court. Jennet, gaining in confidence, provided more and more background information as the trial progressed. She gave evidence against her brother James, among others. Amongst those she claimed had been present at the Malking Tower meeting was Alice Nutter, mother of the dead Robert Nutter. Jennet claimed that her mother had told her that Alice was a witch.

Alice Nutter was a woman of substance, having money and land. To verify the identification Judge Bromley had Jennet taken out of the court while Mrs. Nutter was placed in a group of people. On being brought in again Jennet had no difficulty in identifying her. This was taken as proof of her guilt, regardless of the fact that Jennet was extremely familiar with Alice Nutter outside the court, as well as having been opposite her inside the court immediately prior to the identification.

Some years later, in 1634, Jennet Device was to be herself accused of witchcraft by a child, in the trial of the Pendle Witches.

CHAPTER 6

...NEW ENGLAND

verdict and death-warrant. The Rev. John Norton, the persecutor of Quakers, is on record as having said that Ann Hibbins was hanged "only for having more wit than her neighbors". This wit took her to the gallows on Boston Common in 1656.

In 1688 came the case of the Goodwin children (mentioned briefly in Chapter Two). It involved a Catholic Irishwoman named Glover, who was launderess to the Goodwin household,—John Goodwin and his wife, thirteen-year-old Martha, and three other children aged eleven, seven and five.

One day Martha accused Goody Glover of stealing some linen. The woman broke out in a burst of profanity and curses at the child, who very soon fell down in a fit. The other children quickly followed her example. Then they went through all sorts of pranks. They would pretend to be deaf and dumb, then they would suddenly start barking like dogs. They would try to levitate themselves, moving quickly over the ground on their tip-toes so that Cotton Mather later said they could "fly like geese". They would complain of being pricked by pins.

After a week or two of this behaviour it was decided, among the doctors and ministers who examined them, that they were bewitched by the Glover woman. The Rev. Joshua Moodey wrote from Boston to Increase Mather, father of Cotton, who was then in England. He said "Wee have a very strange thing among us, which we know not what to make of, except it bee Witchcraft, as we think it must needs bee."

In fact they felt so strongly that it "must needs bee" witchcraft that they hanged Goody Glover. Cotton Mather, who had come in contact with the case at quite a late stage, took young Martha Goodwin into his home and kept her there for several months, to study her and treat her both medically and by prayer (Cotton Mather was also a Doctor of Medicine). He said, in *Magnalia*, 1700, "I took her home to my own family, partly out of compassion to her parents, but chiefly that I might be eye-witness of things that would enable me to confute the *Sadducism* of this debauch'd age." He published a full account of the case in his book *Memorable Providences relating to Witchcrafts and Possessions*, Boston, 1689.

The Goodwin children, as later with the children of Salem, knew exactly how a witch was supposed to behave. Tracts and chap-books on the subject were plentiful. The latest trials in England would be published, in detail, and very soon find their way across to the New World.

John Fiske, in *New France and New England*, wrote that, "in 1692, quite apart from any personal influence, there were circumstances which favored the outbreak of an epidemic of witchcraft. In this ancient domain of Satan there were indica-

and Abigail to work, for they were frequently left under her supervision. But the girls were smart; they knew how Tituba loved to talk about her life in the West Indies. They would find it a simple matter to get her to sit at the kitchen table with them, perhaps with young Betty on her knee, and tell them fascinating tales of the islands. Frequently they were not alone, for they could not help boasting to their girl-friends of this prize possession of theirs. The parsonage kitchen very quickly became the regular meeting-place for the village girls. This was especially true during the winter when there was so little to do, for even the festivities of Christmas were denied a Puritan community; it had no place on their calendar.

Exactly what sort of stories Tituba told the children is not known for certain though it is highly probable that they were heavily flavored with tales of voodoo and magic. It is not unlikely that the children would try to re-enact some of these stories perhaps even to the extent of going into trances and uttering mystic words. The group of children included besides Betty and Abigail, Ann Putnam, aged twelve, Mary Walcott and Elizabeth Hubbard, both aged seventeen. There was Elizabeth Booth and Susannah Sheldon, both eighteen, and Mary Warren and Sarah Churchill, both twenty. Occasionally they were also joined by Mercy Lewis, seventeen, a servant in the Putnam household.

Young Ann Putnam rapidly became the leader of the group, despite her age. She had a mother, also named Ann, who was well-educated but very highly strung. This was mainly through losing a number of children at birth before finally bearing the younger Ann. Her sister also had suffered in this way, finally dying in childbirth, and thoughts of those lost were forever in her mind. Her daughter she used as a go-between to try to contact the dead in some way through Tituba.

Early in January 1692 young Betty started to have what could only be described as mild fits. She would stare into space for long periods then, when reprimanded, would cough and splutter and make sounds almost, so Parris said, like the barkings of a dog. Soon Abigail started doing the same, occasionally going to the extent of getting down on all fours and crawling through the furniture. The Reverend Parris prayed over the two girls but since it seemed to do no good he finally took them to the village doctor. Doctor Griggs examined them as well as he was able but could find no reasonable explanation for their behaviour.

Voodoo, as practised in the Caribbean, is a polytheistic religion. It has its priesthood; it has its set forms of worship. One of the tenets of the religion is that the gods, known as *loa*, can manifest themselves by taking possession of the worshippers. The chief deity is Damballah-wedo, who is a serpent god. If a person is possessed, or "ridden" by Damballah then he, or she, will crawl on the ground and hiss like a snake. It is more than likely that Tituba described such possessions to the girls of Salem Village. Thoughts of such possessions may well have played on the mind of young Betty, at that time just nine years old. Not being familiar with snakes she might have imagined being possessed by something she knew well, such as a dog.

Dr. Griggs knew nothing of Tituba's tales, or of voodoo. He shrugged his shoulders in despair and ascribed the whole thing to witchcraft. "Someone" he said, "has obviously bewitched these girls". The Reverend Parris hurried home again with his charges and called in the elders of the village that they might all pray over the girls. No one seemed to notice that whenever they had their "fits" the girls would merely indulge in all the high-spirited things which were normally forbidden to young ladies of such a community. They would shout and scream; they would roll on the floor or jump on the furniture; they would throw things, including the Bible, about the room. In short, they would "have a ball!" It was not long before their friends, those others of the Tituba circle, decided to join in the fun. The village was aghast to suddenly find itself with a half dozen or so hysterical girls on its hands.

This was all very well for a while, but the distressed elders wanted to know who was causing the outbreak. People recalled the case of the Goodwin children. Mather's book on this had received wide circulation. There was probably even a copy of it in the Parris household. Parris called in clergymen from all over the surrounding countryside. They flocked to see the girls, who became known as the "Afflicted Children". The girls for their part must have realised that they had gone too far. To admit that they were shamming would be to lay themselves open to beatings, embarrassment to their elders, to the clergy—it did not bear thinking about. They continued the pretense. But still they were being urged to name who afflicted them.

The Reverend Nicholas Noyes arrived in the village from the First Church in Salem Town. John Hale came from nearby Beverly. Hale had previously dealt with one or two cases of witchcraft in his own area, but had been loath to act against it each time. For the gatherings of ministers the girls would put on a tremendous show. Abigail Williams especially rose to the occasion. Obviously relishing the limelight she would howl louder than all the rest as the clergy tried to pray for them. Since the girls had not been able, apparently, to name who afflicted them the ministers resorted to naming those who had any sort of notoriety in the area, to watch the girls' reaction. It seemed to have no effect. The girls continued their fits, the clergy their prayers.

It could not continue indefinitely. The girls had

to name someone. Finally it was young Betty Parris who mentioned the name of Tituba, though whether she intended it as a charge or not is not known. Parris and the others leapt at the name. *Was* it Tituba? Other girls agreed that it was and, now that names were to be given, added those of Goody Osburn and Goody Goode ("Goody" being short for Goodwife).

Sarah Goode had a bad name in the village. She was virtually a beggarwoman, her husband hiring himself out as a casual laborer. Sarah smoked a pipe, had a quick, coarse tongue, and during a recent smallpox epidemic had been accused of spreading the disease through her general uncleanliness and negligence. She had a number of children and was in fact pregnant at the time of her arrest.

Sarah Osburn was recently bed-ridden but again had no good name in the village. As a widow she had lived with her second husband, William, a number of years before marrying him. With the arrest of these three, and their removal to Ipswich Prison, the village started to breathe again. But it was not to be for long.

* * *

The preliminary hearing, to determine whether or not the case was worthy of a trial, was to be held in the village at Deacon Ingersoll's Ordinary. As it turned out the capacity of the crowd far exceeded that of the Deacon's room so the meeting was held in the church. The magistrates were Jonathan Corwin and John Hathorne, an ancestor of the novelist Nathaniel Hawthorne. Neither of these men had any legal training for the professional practise of law was not permitted in the Puritan colony. Before embarking upon the hearing, therefore, both men perused Cotton Mather's recent work on the Goodwin case and one or two other books such as Bernard's *Guide to Jurymen* and Glanvil's *Collection of Sundry Tryals in England*.

On searching through the Bible they were no doubt nonplussed to find that nowhere in it was there given a definition of witchcraft. In fact the word "witchcraft" itself was hardly used, especially in editions predating King James' version.

The accused were not legally represented in any way, and were presumed guilty before the start. The hearing commenced on Tuesday, March 1st, and the first to be interviewed was Goody Goode. She was openly defiant, disclaiming any knowledge of the affair. Several people testified, however, that there had been times when Goody Goode had come begging and been turned away. On leaving she had been seen to mutter to herself. A day or so later a chicken would have died, or a cow run dry. This seemed proof conclusive.

Goody Osburn was obviously a sick woman. She had been taken from her bed to the prison and now it required assistance to get her to court. She was able to give little in the way of testimony, though whenever she looked at the "Afflicted Children", who were present, they would start going into fits. Finally Goody Osburn was removed and Tituba brought in. This caused a tremendous outburst from the children. It may well have been that they were afraid she would give the full story of the clandestine meetings in the Parris kitchen; that people would put two and two together and decide the girls were pretending. The girls need not have worried.

Tituba rose to the occasion magnificently. Far from claiming innocence she admitted all with which she was charged, and more! For three days she held forth telling her audience everything she felt it wanted to know. Certainly she was a witch, as was Goody Goode and Goody Osburn. She had been approached by a man, a "tall man from Boston", who wanted her to sign her name in his book. Goode and Osburn already had their names in the book. There were, she said, nine names there altogether. This caused quite a stir in the court. If there had been nine names in the book then there were other witches still on the loose, yet to be caught.

The trio was removed to Boston where, a few weeks later, Sarah Osburn died. Goody Goode had the child she was carrying when arrested, but it too died in the cell. Parris' wife insisted on sending Betty to stay with friends in Salem Town, for the fits seemed to be making her weak. This separation from the other girls had the ultimate effect of curing her of her possession.

John Proctor managed, briefly, to cure his servant Mary Warren of her affliction. His method was to set her to her work and promise her a beating if she left it for one moment, fits or no fits! He was most perturbed when Mary was finally called back to court, over his protests, by the magistrates. The elders and ministers had returned to praying over the girls and questioning them regarding the identities of the rest of the witches. It was not long before Ann Putnam provided the name of Martha Corey, an outspoken woman who had moved to the village from Salem Town only a year previously. The main reason for suspicion, in her case, seems to have been her outright—and outspoken—disbelief in witchcraft. When brought before the magistrates Martha started out firmly denying all and saying that the girls should be ignored. But everything that Martha did the girls copied. If she bit her lip they would bite theirs till the blood ran, and say that she caused them to do it. One of the girls claimed to be able to see "the Black Man" standing beside the woman and whispering in her ear.

The next to be "cried out upon" by the girls—

once again led by Ann Putnam—was the aged, extremely deaf, Rebecca Nurse. Rebecca was in her seventies and had for almost a year been ill and confined to her bed. Her whole life, however, she had been regarded as one of the most respected of women, a veritable pillar of the community, a staunch and ever-devout Christian. The main charge against her had been that while she lay seemingly immobile in her bed, her "shape"—her etheric double— was dashing about the community wreaking havoc. Or so claimed the "Afflicted Children". At Rebecca's trial a paper was produced, signed by thirty-nine people, attesting to her good character. It was to have no effect on the final outcome.

The children had their usual fits whilst Rebecca was being questioned. At one point, when Magistrate Hawthorne seemed affected by her straightforward answers, Ann Putnam senior cried out "Did you not bring the Black Man with you? Did you not bid me tempt God and die? How often have you eaten and drunk your own damnation?" Rebecca raised her hands to heaven in despair and the girls took this as a signal to have violent fits. Hathorne decided that it was Rebecca's raised hands that had caused the fits and she was sent to jail to await trial.

Thereafter arrests went on with increasing rapidity until, by the end of the spring, at least one hundred twenty-five people were in prison.

Among these were John Procter and George Jacobs, masters to two serving-girls who were among the "afflicted". John Willard was another. He had said that it was the girls who were the real witches and deserving of the gallows. He was instantly cried out upon.

Perhaps the most amazing arrest was that of the Reverend George Burroughs. He had been minister in Salem Village from 1680 to 1682, and had left there because of various feuds within its church. To his later sorrow he had been on the opposite side of the feud to the senior Ann Putnam. He had settled in Wells, Maine, and was arrested there at the beginning of May and taken to Salem to answer the charge of witchcraft. In a prior consultation with other ministers it came out that he had only had his eldest son baptized and that he could not remember when he had last served the Lord's Supper. Damning evidence. He was stripped and searched for the Devil's Mark, but without success.

By the middle of May the first royal governor, Sir William Phips, had arrived with a new charter, replacing the provisional government of Massachusetts that had followed the overthrow of Andros. On Sir William Phips then departing again for a few months a special court of Oyer and Terminer* was appointed to try the witchcraft cases. This was presided over by William Stough-

*meaning—"To hear and to determine".

ton who, with Samuel Sewall, joined Hathorne and Corwin.

The evidence brought against Burroughs came mainly from Ann Putnam. He was charged, among other things, with murder—but of a "spectral" nature. Apparently whenever a soldier from the village had died in the Indian-fighting he, Burroughs, had actually been responsible. His first two wives appeared—in ghostly form, visible only to the children—to testify that he had murdered them. Burroughs had always been unusually strong for his size and this was now held against him. Whereas he used to take pride in such a feat as that he "held out a gun of seven feet barrel with one hand, and had carried a barrel full of cider from a canoe to the shore," all this was now brought as evidence of his dealing with the supernatural.

One of the tests given to the witches was the test of touch. As the "afflicted" writhed and screamed the accused would be made to touch them. If their screaming then ceased it was proof of guilt for the evil had returned, if only momentarily, to the accused. This test was frequently carried out and unfailingly proved the guilt of the one involved.

* * *

On June 2nd Bridget Bishop became the first of the accused to actually go to trial. Since her original hearing she had been chained up in a prison cell, seeing more and more of the accused join her. One of these was little Dorcas Goode, the five-year-old daughter of Sarah. She, too, had been cried out upon by the girls and she, too, was chained as was the custom with witches.

Although the original examinations had been, supposedly, mere preliminary hearings the evidence from them was carefully reviewed and noted by the magistrates of the Court. The only new business was the hearing of anything fresh which had been uncovered since that time. Bridget Bishop had been a tavern-keeper, having two ordinaries, one at Salem Village, the other in Salem Town. The main charge against her seems to be that she wore a "red paragon bodice" and had a great store of laces. The "new" evidence against her was that she seemed to keep her youth despite her years. Various supposedly decent, upright, married men of the community testified that she sent her "shape" to plague their sleep at night!

The afflicted testified that Bridget had been at the Sabbat meetings of the witches and had, in fact, given suck to a familiar in the form of a snake. She was taken out and searched for a supernumerary nipple, which they claimed to find between "ye pupendum and anus". The verdict was a foregone conclusion. On June 10 Bridget Bishop was hanged on Gallows Hill.

There was a break then of twenty-six days while the judges argued the pros and cons of accepting spectral evidence,—the evidence of the afflicted saying that they saw the shape of the accused in a certain place when physically they were elsewhere. The concensus of opinion was that the devil *could* assume the shape of innocent people (this had previously been doubted) as well as the guilty.

Rebecca Nurse's case soon came up and the jury returned a verdict of Not Guilty. There was immediately a great uproar and the judges expressed their dissatisfaction with the verdict. The foreman of the jury later wrote, on a certificate, "When the verdict not guilty was given, the honored court was pleased to object against it, saying to them, that they think they let slip the words which the prisoner at the bar spoke against herself, which were spoken in reply to Goodwife Hobbs and her daughter, who had been faulty in setting their hands to the devil's book, as they had confessed formerly. The words were, 'What do these persons give in evidence against me now? They used to come among us!' After the honored court had manifested their dissatisfaction of the verdict, several of the jury declared themselves desirous to go out again, and thereupon the honored court gave leave; but when we came to consider the case, I could not tell how to take her words as evidence against her, till she had a further opportunity to put her sense upon them, if she would take it . . . these words were to me a principle evidence against her."

So after having their verdict of not guilty rejected the jurors retired once more and came back with a verdict of guilty. Rebecca tried to explain that when she had referred to Deliverance Hobbs—who had previously confessed to being a witch, though later she joined the ranks of the afflicted—as being "one of us" she did not mean "one of us *witches*" but "one of us *prisoners*"! It was to no avail. Earlier she had damned herself, due to her deafness. She had not answered one of the questions put to her. She had just not heard it. But her silence was taken as acknowledgement of guilt. The Reverend Noyes excommunicated her and Tuesday, 19 July, in company with Sarah Goode, Elizabeth How, Sarah Wild and Susanna Martin, she was hanged on Gallows Hill.

On August 19 the cart driven out to Gallows Hill carried five more: John Procter, John Willard, Martha Carrier, George Jacobs Senior, and the Reverend George Burroughs. Burroughs had been identified by the Afflicted Children as the "Black Man" in charge of the coven. He was allowed to address the crowd from the scaffold. This he did in carefully chosen words which worked on the emotions of the crowd. So much so, in fact, that some started to call for his release. One of the tests of a witch was that he, or she, could not say the Lord's Prayer without blundering. George Burroughs stood at the scaffold and, clearly and faultlessly, recited it to the crowd. Almost certainly they would have released him but, as some moved forward, a young man on a horse cried out to them to stop. It was Cotton Mather. With stern words he cautioned them against the workings of the Devil, intimating that it had been the Devil speaking to them through Burroughs. The hanging went on as planned.

On Monday 19 September an unusual execution was carried out. When a man is brought before the court for trial he is first required to plead whether he is guilty or not guilty. No trial can proceed until the accused has so pleaded. By refusing to plead, therefore, the accused can prevent the trial altogether. To circumvent such an occurence the law provided a horrible punishment for anyone so obstinate. This was called *peine fort et dure*, which means, literally, "a penalty harsh and severe". It consisted of stretching the culprit out flat on his back, with his arms and feet extended to the utmost in four directions. Heavy weights of iron and stone were then piled on the body till he either pleaded, or died. The common name for this process was "pressing to death".

Giles Cory was arrested for witchcraft in April. His wife, who had been in jail since March, was sentenced to death on September 10, and his own trial came two or three days later. In all his eighty years Giles had never known the meaning of fear, yet seeing what was done to his wife nearly broke his heart. He knew that if he did not plead not only would his trial be baulked but also the authorities would be unable to confiscate his goods and estate, as they would be able to do should he be proven guilty. Giles therefore refused to plead and was, subsequently, put to the *peine forte et dure*—the only time in American history that this punishment was inflicted.

Eventually the accusers went too far. They started mentioning members of the Mather family; they tried to implicate Lady Phips, wife of the governor; they named the most respected Rev. Samuel Willard and, finally, Mrs. Hale wife of John Hale himself. This was too much. These accusations opened the eyes of John Hale to the point where he turned right about and began to oppose the whole prosecution. He confessed that he had been wrong all along. It seemed that a number of other people had reached similar conclusions. More and more ministers came out with Hale against the prosecutions. The court recessed.

A fatal blow to the witch-hunters came when a group of people in Andover, on being accused of witchcraft, retorted by bringing an action of defamation of character with heavy damages. This marked the end of the panic. Just at this time the court of Oyer and Terminer was abolished due to the assembly of the General Court of Massachusetts at Boston. It was the first court elected under the new charter. The jail at Salem was filled with prisoners and many had been taken to other jails. When the court met for the first time in January 1693, it started by throwing out indictments. The grand jury found bills against about fifty for witchcraft, but upon trial they were all acquitted. Some of the court were dissatisfied but the juries changed sooner than the judges.

In May, 1693, Governor Phips ordered the release from jail of all those awaiting trial and the Salem witchcraft hysteria was past. Excommunications were erased and claims from survivors and those who had been held from days to months, awaiting trial and almost certain death, were honored by the colony within a few years.

Five years afterwards Judge Samuel Sewell stood up in the Old South Church and publicly acknowledged his shame and repentance. For the rest of his life he kept a day of fasting and prayer, every year, in memory of his errors. Ann Putnam, the younger, fourteen years afterwards, stood before the congregation of Salem Village church and confessed that she, and others, had been the cause of bringing upon the village the guilt of innocent blood, "though what was said and done by me against any person, I can truly and uprightly say before God and any man, I did not out of any anger, malice, or ill-will to any person, for I had no such thing against one of them, but what I did was ignorantly, being deluded of Satan. And particularly as I was a chief instrument of accusing Goodwife Nurse and her two sisters, I desire to lie in the dust and to be humbled for it, in that I was a cause, with others, of so sad a calamity to them and their families."

* * *

What happened in the little village of Salem, where nineteen people were hanged and one man pressed to death, was as nothing to what happened in Europe throughout the persecutions. It has been estimated that as many as nine million people died on the charge of witchcraft during that time.

The ways of witchcraft, in the eyes of the Church, were terrible indeed. But were they really the ways of witchcraft? Or was the Church, the voice of authority, as misguided as those Puritans of New England? Let the second part of this book give the other side—the witches' point of view.

Goddess Figurine, Gloucester, England.

PART II

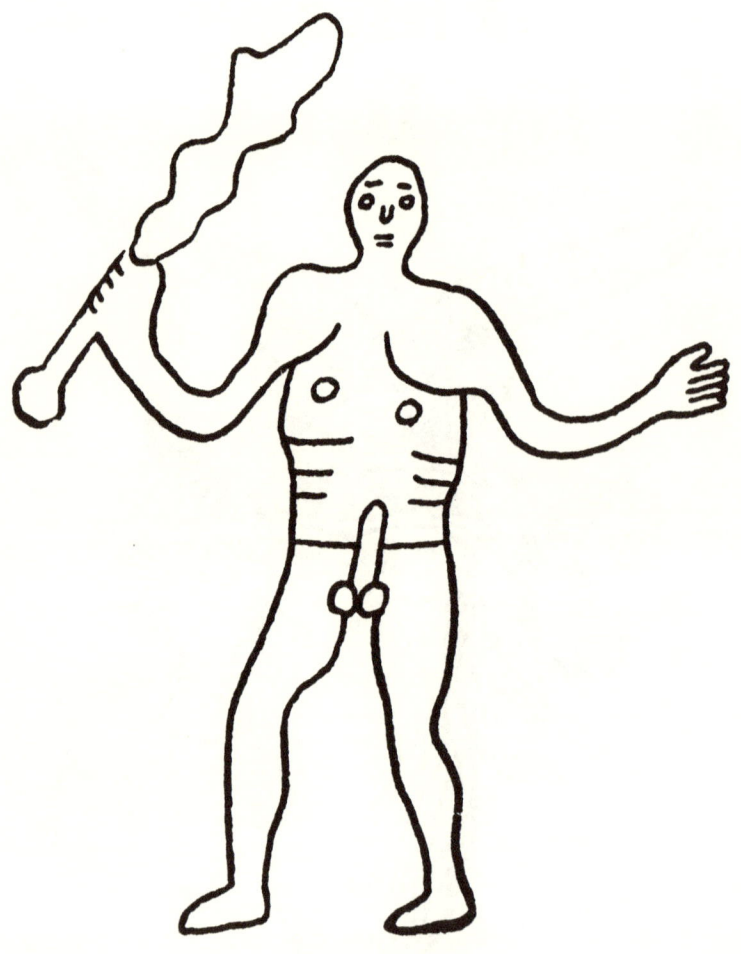

The Cerne Giant, Dorset, England.

CHAPTER 7

INTO SHARPER FOCUS

For hundreds of years, from the very beginning of the printed word, we had been told that witchcraft was something bad. It was involved with black magic, with worship of the Devil, with all things black and evil. There had been periods when it was the fashion to disbelieve that it had ever existed; the late eighteenth/early nineteenth century, for instance, saw a rash of books disclaiming witchcraft. But even these were disclaiming the same type of witchcraft—the bad, the black and the ugly. Whether it really had happened or whether it had all been "in the mind" one thing seemed certain, that it was a product of the early Middle Ages. This was, after all, as we have seen, the time of the start of the persecutions.

In 1921 a new note was sounded. For the very first time a fresh idea of what witchcraft might really have been was presented. It was presented by Dr. Margaret Alice Murray, a distinguished anthropologist and Egyptologist of renown. What Dr. Murray suggested was that witchcraft not only did exist but had existed for centuries, if not millennia, prior to the Middle Ages and the persecutions. More than this she suggested that witchcraft was actually a *religion*. Not a religion of evil, working against the Church, but a pre-Christian religion in its own right, with its own gods, its own priesthood, its own rites and ceremonies.

In the eighteenth century Girolamo Tartarotti had tried to say a little of what Murray said, but had spoken with insufficient authority and with too shallow research to be taken seriously. Murray approached the subject as an anthropologist. It seemed no one had done this before. As Pennethorne Hughes says, "her anthropological approach was the best thing that had happened for generations to what had become folk-lore." She studied the many and various records of witch trials and began to find in them isolated clues that seemed to show witchcraft to be a survival of a pre-Christian religion. She found an odd comment, for example, in a trial in Scotland which was not important to that particular trial. But she would find the same, or similar, comment cropping up in a trial in, say, the south of France. Small points which, when viewed collectively, indicated much.

Dr. Murray published her findings in a book called *The Witch Cult in Western Europe*, in 1921. In this book she dealt specifically with trial records showing, from them, why she reached the conclusions she did. Some years later, in 1931, she followed up with another book, *God of the Witches*, in which she traced the religion back to its probable origins in Palaeolithic times.

This fresh, unbiased approach of Murray's was widely acclaimed by other scholars. The general feeling seems to have been "Why didn't someone the facts and rejected the opinions. The rites she found to be shown as joyous in essence. It was an extremely happy religion and so was in many ways incomprehensible to "the gloomy Inquisitors and Reformers who suppressed it."

Since fertility was of great importance in the old days—fertility of crop and beast—there were certain sexual rites enacted by the followers of what was essentially a nature religion. These sexual rites seem to have been given unnecessary prominence by the Christian judges who seemed to delight in prying into the minutest details concerning them.

The organization of the Craft, throughout Europe, was really the same with only slight local variations. Cotton Mather commented "The witches are organized like Congregational Churches." So it almost seemed. There was a group, within the coven, known as the Elders; just as in the church. There was a leader of the rites, a Priest or Priestess. And there was someone, the Maiden, to stand-in in the absence of the Priestess. The covens themselves were autonomous.

There were, of course, those who could not accept Murray's theories. Montague Summers for one had so steeped himself in the thinking of the church of the Middle Ages that he could not get past the *Malleus Maleficarum*. Elliot Rose, in *A Razor for a Goat*, made an unsuccessful attempt to refute Murray's findings but tripped over his own arguments. One of his criticisms was that Murray and others got their evidence from contemporary pamphlets. He then went on to do exactly the same thing himself to gather evidence for his points! He completely missed Murray's point regarding the forming of the Order of the Garter (see Chapter 8), and shows such reverse reasoning as "I will suggest . . . that perhaps one of the reasons why 'Dianus' was better filled to compete with the God of the Christians was that he had been designed and discovered with that competition in mind"!

Pennethorne Hughes seemed to think that there was some substance to the talk of Black Masses and Devil-worship but, as Gerald Gardner was to point out, "Most of what he says is simply not true . . . the rites are simple, and with a purpose, and in no way resemble those of the Roman Catholic or any other church that I know."

Dr. Gerald Brousseau Gardner was the man to finally complete the picture. In 1949 he wrote a novel, under the pseudonym *Scire*, called *High Magic's Aid*. It was about Ceremonial Magic and Witchcraft as Murray had described it. It was not until 1954, however, that he was able to write the non-fictional *Witchcraft Today*. By that time the last laws against witchcraft, in England, had finally been repealed. He was therefore able to say, in effect, "What Murray and the others have suggested is fact. Witchcraft *was* a religion—and it still is. I know, because I am a witch!" At last a witch had come forward to give the Craft's side of the story.

CHAPTER 8
SPOKES OF THE WHEEL

Gerald Gardner was an anthropologist and archaeologist. Living many years in the Far East he was responsible for the discovery of the site of the ancient city of Singapura (the original city of Singapore), and was a member of Sir Flinders Petrie's dig at Gaza. As an authority—if not *the* authority—on weapons of the Far East he was awarded an honorary doctorate, by the University of Singapore, after publication of his work *Kris, and Other Malay Weapons*, still the standard work on the subject.

In the many years he spent in the areas he made friends with the Iban headhunters, the Saghai Dyaks of Borneo, the Saki pygmies and many other natives never before befriended by whiteman. Interested in magic from his very earliest years Gardner collected details of their beliefs and practises and, whenever possible, actual magical artifacts.

It was not until he was once more living permanently in England, in the 1930s, that Gardner came into contact with witchcraft. An ancestress of his, Grizell Gairdner, had been burned as a witch at Newborough, Scotland, in 1640. He happened to mention this to some people with whom he was acquainted as part of an amateur theatrical group. They showed great interest and it was not long before Gardner found himself going through a ritual, with them, in a large deserted house. The ritual, he quickly realised, was an initiation ceremony. He had finally been made a witch.

A whole new world opened up to Gerald Gardner. His lifelong study of magic held him in good stead. In 1950 he purchased an old windmill and outbuildings dating from 1600, on the Isle of Man. The buildings he adapted to house his huge collection of magical artifacts. (The Isle of Man is a small island in the middle of the Irish Sea). So began the world's first museum of magic and witchcraft.*

Realising that after so long in hiding witchcraft was finally dying out, and feeling that the coven to which he now belonged was probably one of the last in existence, Gardner asked permission to put into writing some of the truth about witchcraft. He was told he should not. Finally, however, he was allowed to write a little, in fictional form, in *High Magic's Aid*. It took five years more to persuade the witches to let him publish *Witchcraft Today*. He wrote this simply to give the true facts while they were still to be had.

In *Witchcraft Today* Gardner says "an anthropologist's job is to investigate what people do and what they believe, not what moralists say they should do and believe." He was amazed, on publishing the book, to receive letters from all over the country, indeed all over western Europe, from other covens. Each one of these had been thinking,

*This was the inspiration, for the author to start *his* Museum of Magic and Witchcraft.

as had Gardner, that their's was probably the last coven in existence, and each was delighted to find there were others still alive. At the time of the persecutions it had been stated, within witchcraft, that no coven must know the whereabouts of another. In this way if one coven was captured it could not give away another. So it was that the covens had all lost touch with one another. Now it was to be Gardner's lot to act as a clearinghouse for the Craft. Studying all he could and collecting, as always, books and artifacts, Gardner naturally became the "Grand Old Man" of the witch world. There is no One Leader in witchcraft; no King of the Witches. Yet Gardner became the *un*official father figure, the voice of authority; the witchcraft spokesman.

From the incredible number of letters he received from all over the world he found hundreds of people wanting information, or wanting to join the Craft. Virtually all said that this was the very type of religion they had been searching for all their lives. In 1959 *The Meaning of Witchcraft*, a complementary volume to his previous one, was published.

* * *

As Gardner explains, witchcraft is what would be called a Mystery Religion. Many parallels may be found between it and the ancient Greek and Roman Mysteries. The center point of any such

Bronze Horned God Figure, Denmark.

initiation is the symbolical death and rebirth. To be reborn; to start life anew in the new religion. To go with this rebirth many people take a new name. A list of suitable names from which they may choose is usually kept by the High Priestess. This list is made up of names from Celtic mythology and Greek mythology, names of witches of the past taken from records of the trials, and just plain "witch-sounding" names. If the person to be initiated has her own idea of what name she wants—she may decide to keep her given name—then that is quite acceptable.

Another important point in any initiation is the oath of secrecy. It is precisely what its name implies—it is a promise to keep, for ever, the secrets of the Craft, the religion. It does not include any repudiation of a previous religion. It seems possible that such a repudiation was included over a period during, and leading up to, the persecutions. This was almost certainly designed to ensure that spies from the New Religion were not infiltrating the Craft with a view to exposing it. As I say there is no repudiation included in the ceremony today. Also there is no kissing of goat's buttocks or trampling or spitting on a cross!

Incidentally the idea of a cross being a charm against witchcraft (on the false assumption that witchcraft is evil) is nonsense, for the cross was a religious symbol long before it was adopted by

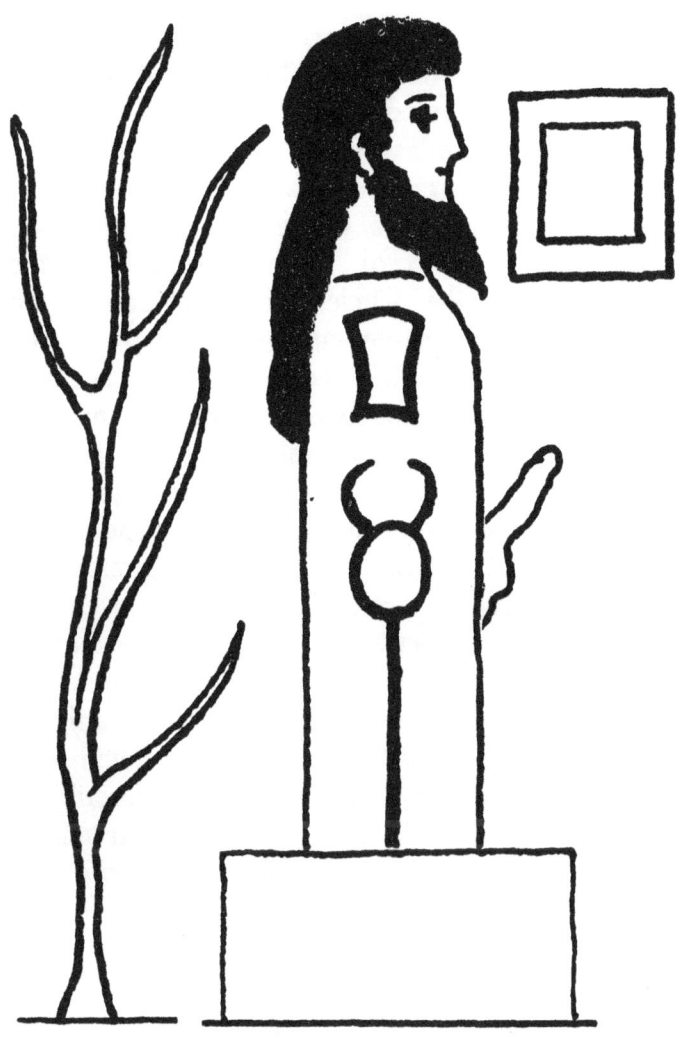

Greek Vase Painting of Fertility God.

Christianity. It was already in use in eastern Europe in the Bronze Age. Originally it was, as a cross with extended ends, a symbol for the sun. The extended ends would frequently meet to form a circle with the cross enclosed.

All meetings of a coven (the name for an established group of witches) start with the "casting" of the Circle. The initiation is no exception. Before the initiate is brought in the High Priestess will take the coven sword (she may use her *athame*, the witch's personal knife, in lieu of the sword) and walk around in a circle to mark the meeting place. In the days when covens could gather out in the open she would stick the point of the sword into the ground and literally draw the circle. Today, when covens are more likely to meet in a house, the circle may be painted on the floor, or designated by the laying out of a white cord, or drawn temporarily in chalk. Yet even so the High Priestess will start the proceedings by walking around "describing" the circle. She will then consecrate this circle. When all the preliminaries have been carried out then will the neophyte be brought in.

Gerald Gardner describes the Initiation Room at the Villa of Mysteries, in Pompeii. This was the one place in Italy where *everyone*, including slaves, would go to be initiated into the Dionysian Mysteries. Around the walls of this room, which the author visited not long ago, are frescoes depicting a woman going through this ceremony. It says much for the respect of the followers for their Oath of Secrecy in that very little is known today about this religion. Only what we can gather from the paintings around the walls. As Gardner said, a witch could look at these paintings and recognise several points which are found in a witchcraft initiation.

The frescoes show a woman going through the ceremony. The High Priestess in the scenes has been identified as the woman who actually owned the villa. Again even this fits with witchcraft in that the meetings of a coven are invariably held at the home of the High Priestess.

Being basically a religion of nature witches always work in pairs, one male and one female. In the same way that everywhere in nature you must have male and female. When a man is initiated into the Craft he is brought in by the High Priestess; when a woman comes in it is by the High Priest.

The initiation is divided into four main parts: the Challenge, the Ordeal, the Oath, and the Showing of Tools. The Challenge takes place when the neophyte is first brought to the Circle. Before stepping into it he is confronted by the High Priestess who asks him, in essence, if he really does want to go through with it. On saying that he does he will be blindfolded and bound then taken into the Circle in a certain manner. He is led around to the four cardinal points and presented to the gods as a person wishing to be initiated.

It is the blindfolding which is the "ordeal". To not know exactly where you are, to be led about turned this way and that, and not to know just what to expect next can be a very real ordeal. Its symbolism, together with the binding, is of course the restriction of the womb prior to birth, and is found the world over.

The "death" is symbolized with a scourging. This is a ritual scourging, it is *not* a "whipping" —it is very definitely *not* to hurt. Again this scourging, which is basically a purification, a cleansing, is found the world over and is one indication of the antiquity of witchcraft.

The Oath is read by the High Priestess, line by line, to the neophyte who repeats it after her. Once it is taken the blindfold may be removed. In the Initiation into Freemasonry there is a phrase which goes: "To all this (the oath of the first degree) and these I solemnly and sincerely promise and swear without equivocation, mental reservation, or secret evasion in me whatever, binding myself under no less penalty than having my throat cut end to end, my tongue torn out by its roots, and my body buried in the rough sands of the sea, a cabletow length from shore, where the tide ebbs and flows twice in twenty-four hours, should I knowingly and willingly violate this my solemn obligation . . ." In Freemasonry this is no idle threat, as a certain Captain Morgan, of Bavata, New York, found in 1826 when he was kidnapped and cruelly murdered for daring to publish the secrets of the Masons.

In witchcraft, there are no such dire threats. There is no fear that some mysterious man dressed all in black is going to follow you through the streets; no horrible curse hanging over your head. Yet never has the oath been broken.

The next important part of the Initiation is the Showing of the Tools. Each coven has a set of "working tools", which are kept on the altar standing in the center of the Circle. I have mentioned the sword, which is one of the tools. Another is the Wand. This is not a magic wand in the sense that it can be waved to turn a pumpkin into a golden coach! It has certain ritual uses. There is one tool owned by all witches. This is the *Athame*. Each witch has her own personal athame, which is small, black-handled knife with a straight, double-edged blade. On the handle are carved certain signs and, as with the other tools, it has been consecrated. This is never used for any physical cutting in the Circle. There are no blood sacrifices performed.

As each of the eight tools is shown to the Initiate the High Priestess explains in what way it is used. To signify that he understands the explanation given the Initiate gently places both his hands on the tool for a moment. At the end of the Initiation the High Priestess leads the new witch around the circle again to the four cardinal points. At each one he is presented to the gods as a "newly initiated Priest and Witch".

* * *

A question frequently asked is "But how do I get to be initiated?" The first step is to make contact with a coven, the second is to prove that you are of the right material for witchcraft. Of these two the first is generally the most difficult. There are many spurious covens about these days (which will be looked at in Chapter 12), so the sincere seeker needs to be wary. Many people make their initial contact through the author of a worthwhile book on witchcraft. When Gerald Gardner was alive (he died in February, 1964) people would write to him, in care of his publisher, and he would see that the letter was eventually forwarded to the coven closest to the writer. Much the same thing is done today. (In fact any reader of this book who is sincerely interested in the Craft as a religion is invited to write to the author—who is a High Priest and was, in fact, originally initiated by Gerald Gardner's High Priestess—I will see that the letter eventually reaches the coven existing closest to the writer) I say "eventually" because there may be many reasons why no reply is forthcoming by return.

The God of The Witches, from an Old Wood Carving.

One such reason is simply a test of interest. If you write enthusiastically asking to be put in touch with a coven and then hear nothing for, perhaps, six months how enthusiastic will you be feeling then? If it is an enthusiasm for the Old Gods that cannot last half a year what likelihood is there of your *really* desiring the Craft? This is not to say that you will have to wait that long for an answer, but it is possible.

Once contact is made there will be a necessarily long "feeling-out" period. By its history of misrepresentation witchcraft does attract many people for the wrong reasons. People who think that witchcraft is Satanism, that it is tantamount to wild sex orgies, to blood sacrifices and the like, are likely to want to join. Usually once they find out that they are mistaken, that witchcraft is actually rather "tame", they disappear by themselves. But to safeguard the Craft from people with such misconceptions the waiting period has to be long. The recommended period is "one year and one day".

During this time, of course, there is much contact between the would-be witch and the coven. It may start with an exchange of letters but will soon reach the point of meeting together in person. The initial meeting, on the side of the coven, may be by the High Priestess herself, by her High Priest, or by a representative. Eventually, however, you will meet with all members of the coven.

The keyword to acceptance into a coven is "sincerity". Sincerity in believing in the Old Gods and in wanting to worship them. Remember always that it is the religion which is first and foremost. Any "magic" is always secondary. If it is magic which is your prime interest you do not necessarily need the Craft. The practise of Ceremonial Magic may be more in your line.

Once initiated it is within everyone to become a High Priest or High Priestess. There is, in the Craft, a system of degrees of advancement. You are initiated into the First Degree. Many people are content to remain there. They want to *belong* yet do not want to go on to the point of accepting responsibility. There is nothing wrong with this. If, however, you do wish to advance you will learn, basically by doing. The High Priestess will keep her eye on you in the Circle to see how you are progressing, and to teach and encourage you in whatever she feels is your strong-point. She it is who decides when you are ready for the Second Degree. Again it is suggested that at least a year and a day should elapse from the passing of the First Degree. But this is not mandatory. It could be less time than that, though it is unusual, or it could be much longer. The same period of time is suggested between Second and Third Degree.

The Third Degree is the highest, in witchcraft. When at this degree you are considered to be one of the Elders of the coven. You are consulted on matters of coven policy. In the old days there might have been several elders in the coven. It was from these that the High Priestess would pick her High Priest. It has been said that a coven must consist of thirteen people. This is not so. Thirteen is the traditional maximum number but is certainly not mandatory. It can be any number from two to two thousand (if you could fit them in the nine foot circle), together with the High Priestess who must always be present. It is, indeed, the physical size of the circle that commands the numerical size of the coven. By tradition the diameter of the circle is nine feet. At its center stands the Altar. It can straightway be seen, then, that the number of people who can stand or sit within that space with any degree of comfort is strictly limited. A dozen is maximum; eight or ten give you just that much more elbow-room.

In the old days, when most covens had the maximum, the High Priestess would choose any male of the Third Degree to act as her High Priest. She might pick one man at one meeting, a different man at the next. For the ceremonial parts of the meetings the man's female partner would sit outside the Circle, thus leaving the necessary equal numbers of male and female within. These days the High Priestess usually has a permanent High Priest, because when a woman reaches the Third Degree she is encouraged to break away and form a new coven. Thus is witchcraft trying, gradually, to get back on its feet.

When a witch breaks away, in this way, she becomes a High Priestess in her own right. Any other members of the original coven may also break away to become members of the new. This is usually done when the joining of the new coven means belonging to a more easily accessable coven, geographically. No witch may be a regular member of more than one coven, though it is quite possible to visit others. The original High Priestess will assist the new High Priestess in every way, perhaps presenting her with all the necessary tools. This original High Priestess now becomes known as a Witch Queen. She rules her own coven and also the new one, though she would never interfere—she is really just there for help and advice when needed. There are, therefore, a number of Witch Queens—High Priestesses with more than one coven. But since covens are autonomous, there can be no one Queen of *all* witches.

As a "badge of office" a High Priestess wears a special bracelet. It is a flat, wide silver one with certain signs engraved on it. The High Priest also wears a bracelet, though his is a little different, being of hammered brass or, if he is lucky, gold. The Queen also has her symbols of rank. She wears a crown, which is a simple band of silver with a silver crescent moon at the front. She also wears a garter of green leather (NOT, as Hans Holzer once described it, a "garter-belt"!) on which are small silver buckles—one for each coven over which she rules. Should you meet a Witch Queen (such as the greatly respected Lady Rowen, of New York) who wears a garter bearing a large number of buckles, you can be sure she has been in the Craft some years and has well earned the respect paid her.

In witchcraft the woman is held in higher esteem than the man. The High Priestess is more important than the High Priest. In fact a meeting may be held without a High Priest being present, but could never be held without the High Priestess.

* * *

Dr. Margaret Murray brought out a most interesting point regarding the ancient English order of chivalry, the Order of the Garter. The story of its formation, according to most history books, is as follows. The Countess of Salisbury was attending a ball held by King Edward III. It was 1350—a time when England was still partly pagan, though nominally Christian. At the ball were many dignitaries of the Church. As the Countess danced with the king she happened to drop her garter. To avoid embarrassment the king picked it up and put it on his own leg, with the words *Honi soit qui mal y pense* ("Shame be to him who thinks ill of it"). He later went on to form the Order of the Garter as an order of chivalry.

Murray points out that it took more than a dropped garter to embarrass a lady in those days, even a Countess dancing with a king. What would have been embarrassing, however, particularly in view of the Church dignitaries being present, would have been if the garter had been a ritual one. It seems more than likely that this was so and, in putting it on his own leg, Edward made a very smart move. What he did, in effect, by this action was to proclaim himself willing to lead the pagan population as well as the Christian. It is significant that in forming the Order he formed it of twenty-four knights together with himself and the Prince of Wales—twenty-six in all, or twice times thirteen. As head of the Order the king wore a cloak over which were scattered one hundred sixty-eight miniature garters. Together with the one on his leg would be one hundred sixty-nine, or thirteen times thirteen.

The words of the king, on picking up the fallen garter, seem to mystify some. I would suggest that when he said "Shame be to him who thinks evil of it" the "it" to which he referred was the Craft—the Old Religion. Then his words would make remarkable sense.

* * *

A coven comprises a general cross-section of people. Housewives, clerks, teachers, storekeepers, soldiers, sailors, airmen, university professors, opera-singers, writers, etc., etc. The one thing they have in common is that they are what might be termed "thinking people". They are people who do not just accept something because other people have accepted it, or because their parents did it and their parents before them. They are the sort who will study a subject from all angles before attempting to reach a verdict on it.

Witchcraft is a great equalizer. Witches look upon themselves as being like the spokes of a wheel; no one is either first or last, all are equal. This is also emphasized in the mode of worship. Witches worship naked—*skyclad* as they, rather picturesquely, term it. No one can turn up dressed "to kill" and make someone else feel inferior. No one attends meetings just to show off a new dress or a new hat. Nakedness is a tremendous equalizer.

Witchcraft is very much a religion of participation, as I believe all religions should be. Rather than being a place where you are virtually a member of an audience, in the Circle you are actually "on stage". You are literally taking part in the ceremony. This participation I know means a tremendous amount to many people.

Because of the misconceptions held few witches will admit to being such. For example, a witch who is a school-teacher might find herself out of a job should it be known what her religion is (in spite of the so-called "freedom of religion" in this country), simply because the parents of the children in her charge might feel she was likely to try to convert them or "lead them astray". In actual fact there is no prozelytizing whatsoever in witchcraft. It is felt that those who want the Craft will, eventually, find it. There is no need to try to gain converts.

A witch might lose his job because of his boss' misconceptions. It is said that the persecutions are over but, as one witch pointed out to Gardner, "If it were known in the village what I am, every time anyone's chickens died, every time a child became sick, I should be blamed. Witchcraft doesn't pay for broken windows!" Here, then, is an area where the "witch names" come in handy. As a protection for the coven members. Should the High Priestess need to write to a member of her coven she would start the letter simply "Dear Fian", or whatever the name. She would sign it with her Craft name. The address at the top of the letter would be "The Covenstead" (the home of the coven). In this way should the letter fall into the wrong hands it would have nothing to connect the witch with anything. In some covens the members only know one another by their Craft names, just the High Priestess knowing who they are in everyday life.

A High Priestess is always addressed, by a

Wood Carving of Witch from Gypsy Caravan—1820.

witch, as "My Lady" and is referred to as "The Lady Rowen" or "The Lady Froniga", or whatever her name. A Witch Queen is addressed in the same manner. A High Priest is in his position through being chosen by the High Priestess, as has been explained. Should his High Priestess become a Queen then he will assume the gratuitous title of *Magus*. So there cannot be a Magus without a Queen. There is no such title as "King" in witchcraft, in spite of the claims of some publicity-seekers to be "King of all the Witches"!

An ordinary witch—by this I mean a witch who is not yet a High Priestess—is just called by her Craft name: Deidre, Morag, Theo, etc. There is no prefix of the word "witch". I have encountered one or two pseudo-witches who do give themselves such a prefix. For instance "Witch Lesley", "Witch Arnold", even (believe it or not) a "Witch Hazel"! Since Craft names are only used within the Craft such a prefix is superfluous—another witch knows you are one so why include the word in your name? But more on this later.

Palaeolithic Painting of Man Acting the Part of the God of Hunting.

CHAPTER 9
INGREDIENTS OF WITCHCRAFT

"Once in the month, and better it be when the Moon is full, gather ye in some secret place and adore me who am Queen of all the Witcheries." So runs the exhortation to the witches to gather together, at a certain time, for their worship. They must meet then, at least once a month, and preferably at the Full Moon. These monthly meetings are known as *Esbats*. It is at these that any "work" (using *magic*) will be done. Of course the coven may meet more frequently than that, but certainly not less frequently. Some covens meet every week. This is quite possible, and greatly favored, when all members live fairly close to the Covenstead. *Covenstead* is the name given to the place where the coven meets. Not the actual room, necessarily—which may be called the "Magic Room" or the "Temple"—but the house in which it is located, usually the home of the High Priestess.

The area over which the High Priestess rules, and from which her witches come, is called the *Covendom*. This traditionally extends for one league in all directions from the Covenstead. One league is approximately three miles, so you have a circle with a three mile radius about the Covenstead. It was necessary to lay down such a definite area for, in the old days, it could save one High Priestess from stepping on another's toes. It meant that Covensteads were always at least six miles apart.

Today, in the United States at any rate, such hard and fast boundaries are not necessary for the nearest coven is frequently hundreds of miles away. Eventually, perhaps, the Craft will regain much of its old strength, and then the "one league" line will have more meaning.

* * *

There are thirteen full moons in the year so there are as many Esbats. One of the ceremonies held at such a meeting—indeed the most important Esbat ceremony—is called Drawing Down the Moon. In this the High Priest invokes the Goddess to descend into the body of the High Priestess. Then, through the High Priestess' person, the Goddess will speak to the assembled coven.

In addition to the Esbats there are the festivals known as Sabbats (from the French *s'ebattre*, to revel or frolic). There are eight of these in the year—four Greater Sabbats and four Lesser Sabbats. They are spaced more or less equi-distant throughout the year. The four Greater Sabbats are Samhain (or Hallowe'en), Candlemas, Lammas and Beltane. Of these Samhain and Beltane are the two most important. They are the two that divide the year into winter and summer. Years ago during summer it was easy to live on food grown in the soil. But during the winter, when it was no longer possible to grow things, you had to hunt animals for food.

Margaret Murray points out that such a division of the year accentuates the antiquity of witchcraft. As she says, "The dates of the two chief festivals, May Eve (Beltane) and November Eve (Samhain), indicate the use of a calendar which is generally acknowledged to be pre-agricultural and earlier than the solistial division of the year. The fertility rites of the cult bear out this indication, as they were for promoting the increase of animals and only rarely for the benefit of the crops. The cross-quarter days, February 2 (Candlemas) and August 1 (Lammas), which were also kept as festivals, were probably of later date as, though classed among the great festivals, they were not of so high an importance as the May and November Eves."

The four Lesser Sabbats are the Spring and Autumn Equinox and the Summer and Winter Solstice. On each of the eight Sabbats a different ceremony is performed, appropriate for the time of year. Once or twice the date of a Sabbat may coincide with a full moon. In that case the Esbat becomes a Sabbat, though the Drawing Down the Moon ceremony would still be performed. The Sabbats are looked upon as a time for rejoicing, so no "work" would be done at that meeting unless it was some emergency healing. It is no secret, incidentally, that many of the festivals of the New Religion—Christianity—were based on the older ones.

The gods of witchcraft are many, though there are only two main deities. These two, a god and a goddess, are the only ones who have names (The names are, of course, secret to the initiated). The others are just referred to as "the Gods" or "the Mighty Ones". In some respects they are like the Catholic Saints. The two main deities of the Craft were originally the God of Hunting and the Goddess of Fertility. Twenty-five thousand years or more ago, in the period that is called Palaeolithic, early man believed that there were an almost infinite number of gods. He thought of a God of the Storm; a God of the Sea; of the River, of the Forest; of the Rock. This belief is called *animism*. Of these many gods the one who was most directly concerned with Man was the God of Hunting. After all, without success in the hunt it would be impossible to survive. So Man started to perform ceremonies to placate this god. There is still evidence of this early religio-magic to be found in the caves of France and Spain. In one, the Caverne des Trois Freres, may be seen a painting of one of the first priests. It shows a man dressed in skins and wearing a mask and antlers, like a stag. He was representing the God of Hunting. This god was usually thought of as being horned simply because the majority of the animals hunted were horned.

It was with the coming of agriculture that the fertility Goddess really came into the picture, though she had been in the background before. Fertility was needed not only in the plants but also among the animals and men. The more animals; the more food to hunt. And, with the high rate of death, the more children born into the tribe the better guarantee that the tribe would continue. Since it is the woman who is visibly connected with birth—she is the one who literally brings forth—so the Goddess was finally looked upon as being more important than the God. This became especially true when Man learned not only to grow food but also to store sufficient to last through the winter. In this way there was less need to rely on hunting, and so the God became less a God of Hunting and more a God of Nature. That is how he is regarded today by the witches; also as a god of "death and all that comes after".

The High Priest and High Priestess of a coven are the representatives of this god and goddess. They lead the coven in the worship. I have mentioned that Hallowe'en is the Sabbat which marks the change of the year, from summer to winter. This change meant, in the early days, going back to hunting as the primary method of obtaining food. The emphasis of the worship therefore shifted, at this time of year, from the Goddess to the God. This shift is played out in the witchcraft ceremony of Hallowe'en when the High Priestess takes a horned helmet and crowns the

High Priest with it. From then on, for the next six months, the High Priest as the god will play the leading part in the rituals, many meetings revolving around him.

Hallowe'en is also the time of year when witches especially think of relatives and friends who have died during the previous year. They believe that the spirits of these people come to the Sabbat to celebrate with them. To symbolize this attendance they would, in the old days, carry with them lighted torches. These served the two-fold purpose of lighting the way and of representing the loved one. So that the flames would not be blown out as they travelled the lights would be carried in hollowed-out turnips or pumpkins. From these came the Jack-o'-lantern familiar to all at Hallowe'en.

The Sabbats were not the wild sexual *debacles* believed and described by the Christian chroniclers. At the Sabbats all the covens of one Queen would come together, as they still do today, to celebrate. For some witches it might involve quite a long journey, by old standards, to get to the Sabbat site. They would therefore take food with them—perhaps chickens—and cooking utensils. Finally arriving at the site they would start a fire and cook their food. It was probably easiest to carry just one large general-purpose cooking pot— the cauldron. But it was not unbaptised children cooked in it. It was simply the chicken, together with locally-gathered herbs, berries, nuts, etc. Basically just a family cook-out, distorted out of all proportion by the religion's rival.

There is no fear of death in witchcraft. It is a time for celebration, for one of the main tenets of the religion is a belief in reincarnation. At death there is no separate Heaven and Hell. There is just one place for everyone. This is known as the Summerland. The spirit, or soul, goes to this place—which is ruled over by the God—and there rests and relaxes until, growing young again, it is finally reborn through the agency of the Goddess, in another body. There is no need for a Hell, or a Final Judgement, in witchcraft because of their belief in retribution in the present life. It is thought that whatever you do will return threefold. If you do good then you will receive back three times as much good; but if you do evil, then that too will return at three times the strength. Obviously there is no inducement for a witch to work evil!

Each incarnation, it is thought, is better in some way than the last. It is a progression. You might draw a parallel with a child moving through the grades in a school. In each grade there is a certain amount of work, of learning, that has to be accomplished. Once it is done then you are free to move on to the next grade. There is, of course, a vacation period between the grades. How many incarnations you must go through I do not know.

The Craft was originally an oral tradition. It was not until the start of the persecutions that anything was put into writing and then it was done so that all would not be lost. The book which contains the Craft writings is called the *Book of Shadows*. Its name derives from the time of its innovation. Witches were having to meet in secret, in "the shadows", so their writings took this picturesque title. Unfortunately the book only contains the bare essentials. Theological thoughts are not included, hence we cannot say how many incarnations there are, nor what happens after the final one (it is assumed that at that point you become "at one" with the gods).

The Book of Shadows is kept by the High Priestess. It is definitely not a book which may be purchased in any store. It is handwritten. When a new coven forms the new High Priestess will copy by hand the entire Book of Shadows from her Queen. At one time every witch possessed a book, though only the High Priestess had the complete contents. In these individual books were kept snippets of the Craft Law, words of the chants, details of the dances, and the individual's collection of herb lore, charms, cures, etc. These days it is usual for there to be just the one coven book kept by the High Priestess. After all there is little point in, say, a First Degree witch having all the details of every ceremony. It is just one more thing to be guarded from falling into the wrong hands.

Obviously copying by hand opens up the possibility of error. This is well realised and therefore one of the first things that happens when one coven comes into contact with another for the first time is that they compare their books. In this way when they find a discrepancy the Elders can discuss it and decide which version is more likely to be correct. So the books are once again being brought back into line. Gerald Gardner has a number of quite old Books of Shadows in his collection. The oldest—and probably the oldest existing copy anywhere—dates from the sixteenth century. The New York coven (of Lady Rowen) has brought its Book into line with this old one, as have many English covens.

* * *

The Goddess has a very close affinity with the moon. It is well known that the moon exerts a tremendous influence on many things, including crops. Even today there are a large number of farmers who sow and reap according to the phases of the moon. So it is that this satellite has become so well established as a goddess symbol. But it is no more than a symbol. Witches do not worship the moon in itself, or the sun for that matter. Occasionally the question arises "How do you feel about Man landing on the Moon? Will this affect your beliefs in any way?" The answer is that it has absolutely no effect, simply because

WITCHCRAFT—ANCIENT & MODERN

the Moon is just a *symbol* for the deity.

The metal of the Moon is silver. For this reason the High Priestess' bracelet, and the Witch Queen's crown, is of that metal. The bracelet of the High Priest is the metal of the sun, or the color of that metal—gold.

* * *

The word *magic* has been mentioned and is worthy of explanation. It is another of those words which have different connotations for different people. First of all we are not talking about stage magic—conjuring, or prestidigitation. Pulling rabbits out of hats and sawing young ladies in two is a different type of "magic" entirely. Indeed to differentiate between these two types the magic of witchcraft, and of the occult world generally, is frequently spelled with a final "k"—*Magick*. This is an older spelling and one which many witches prefer.

Aleister Crowley (the so-called "Wickedest Man in the World") defined magic thus: "To cause change to occur in conformity with will". The late Dr. Joseph Kaster put it, "Producing desired results by unnatural methods". Many witches would disagree with Kaster in that the witch methods are, to all intents and purposes, completely natural. Aleister Crowley's definition, if we must have one, would seem to be about the best.

Behind the magic of witchcraft is a belief that "power" comes from the human body. Exactly what constitutes this power is not known and, so far as the witches themselves are concerned, does not matter. All that matters is that it is there and can be used. Witches work naked, or *skyclad*, so that they can draw off as much of this power as possible from all parts of the body. Science has proved conclusively that there are such emanations* and that they come more strongly from some parts of the body than from others.

This power is inherent in all of us; it is not peculiar to witches. It is the basis of E.S.P., of spiritualistic phenomena, of faith-healing, of the ouija board, to name but a few. The witches' secret is in knowing how to bring it out, and bring it out strongly, and how to put it to use. Working within their Circle they can, through certain dances among other methods, draw off a fantastic amount of power. Through its consecration the drawn Circle will contain that power until the High Priestess decides it is the right moment to use it. She will then "direct" it, through the gods, to achieve whatever is necessary. It is usually used for healing.

An example of the use of this power, by witches,

---

*cf. the experiments conducted by Prof. Otto Rahn, at Cornell University.

is the case of the girl who was in a coma for sixty days. She had been using drugs, notably LSD, and had finally suffered a break-down and fallen into a coma from which, after sixty days, she showed no signs of recovering. The girl herself was not a witch—witches, incidentally, do not use drugs of any sort. A friend of the girl went to a witch to ask for aid. This witch in turn advised her coven and it was decided to "do work" for the stricken girl. It is referred to as "work" simply because that is what it is. After performing magic you feel thoroughly exhausted, both physically and mentally.

The coven met and for three consecutive meetings directed their "cone of power", as it is called, to the patient. It was at the height of the third session, so they found later, that the girl suddenly awoke. She came out of the coma reporting that she felt fine and, incredibly enough, has since shown no sign of drug after-effects. She has not gone back to drugs and is now a perfectly normal individual.

Any one example of magic can be explained away by the skeptic as "coincidence". But coincidence is, after all, a very handy word. The witches themselves feel that they have done enough such cases to rule out coincidence. If no one else wants to believe them, it does not matter to them.

The above does not mean that witches do not believe in doctors or hospitals, as with the

Christian Scientists. They feel that a doctor has been specifically trained in healing so obviously he is the person to see when you are ill. But in cases, such as the above, where the medical profession has done all it can and can go no further, then will the Craft try their hand.

There are no food taboos in witchcraft. There are no special diets, vegetarian or other, to be followed. Also there is no equivalent to the Ten Commandments, and no Catechism. The morals of the Craft are the morals of the community in which the person lives. All that matters is that you should "harm none".

Although the directing of the "power" is thought of as being in the form of a cone the true "Cone of Power" (sometimes called the "Grand Cone of Power") is used only in times of national emergency. It is performed with a temporary coven made up of High Priests and High Priestesses led by a Witch Queen. Such a Circle was called together at the time that Hitler was threatening invasion of England. It had been similarly formed against Napoleon and against the Spanish Armada. One of the reasons that the Cone of Power is so seldom used is that the forces produced are so incredibly strong—as they have to be—that invariably by the end of the ritual one of the Circle is dead from exhaustion.

In a recent discussion on witchcraft the question came up "What proof is there that witches always work naked? *Is* this tradition, or is it a recent innovation?"

There are certainly many early illustrations of naked witches annointing themselves preparatory to their departure for the Sabbat, but there are also illustrations of witches *at* the Sabbat who are clothed. For interest I did a little research to see how many, if any, such early illustrations showed the witches actually naked at the Sabbat. The result was fairly conclusive. Hans Baldung Grun, the sixteenth century German, did any number of witch illustrations ("Witches at Work" and "Witches' Sabbat" are typical) all showing naked participants. Albrecht Durer's "The Four Sorcerers" is of naked witches. The Douce Collection, Bodleian Library, Oxford, contains an illustration of "The Witches' Sabbat on the Brocken" with many of the participants naked. Practically all of Goya's paintings of witches show them naked ("Two Witches Flying on a Broom" being typical), and especially interesting is the 1613 (Paris) edition of Pierre de Lancre's *Tableau de l'inconstance des mauvais anges* which shows a great gathering with a circle of dancing nudes in one part and a nude mother presenting her equally naked child to the Horned God in another part.

It would seem, then, that there was no hard and fast rule. As is found today some covens only strip when working magic but otherwise wear loose robes. Other covens are naked throughout their rites.

Roman Altar Stone of Cernnunos
found beneath Notre Dame Cathedral.

CHAPTER 10

HORNS BUT NO TAIL

So the God of the Witches is a horned god, but only because originally he was the God of Hunting. As early Man developed, and gradually spread across Europe and Asia, he took with him his ideas of this god. A God of Hunting; a God of Nature. In different countries he was given different names, but always was he basically the same.

The Romans labelled this god *Cernunnos*, a latin word which simply means "the horned one". There are many existing records of this deity. One such was found under Notre Dame Cathedral, in Paris. It was an ancient altar stone with the name Cernunnos inscribed on it together with a crude picture of the god. The name crops up in many parts of England. In some areas it has been shortened to *Cerne*, while in other areas this has become *Herne*. In fact the ancient god Herne is said to ride through Windsor Great Park, accompanied by his hounds, at every full moon.

Representations of this god are still to be found on old buildings and especially in old churches throughout Europe. When many of these churches were first built the only stone-masons and wood-carvers available to do the work were still followers of the Old Religion. They would include the faces of their gods in the many decorations of the buildings so that later, when they had to go to these churches, they could still worship their own deities there.

It is sometimes said that witches worship "The Great God Pan". This is not so. Pan was actually quite a minor god in ancient Greece. Since he is always depicted as a god with horns he became associated with the god of the Old Religion. He certainly may have been worshipped as the nature deity in that particular area at one particular time, but "Pan" is not the name used by the witches for their god. In England, according to the evidence of the trials, the god was never depicted as goat-headed or goat-horned. This was far more common on the Continent. In England the horns were more often those of a stag.

From very early times horns have been a symbol of deity. They are also a symbol of sexual virility. So a goat or a bull would be regarded as a particularly virile animal, the epitome of masculinity. In ancient Crete the bull was very much in evidence. In Cretan mythology King Minos' wife Pasiphae fell in love with the sacred bull of Crete. She directed Daedalus to make an artificial cow for her, so that she could hide inside it and enjoy the bull when it copulated with the cow. This was done and Pasiphae later produced the Minotaur from that union. The Minotaur was half man, half bull. To hide this insult the king had Daedalus design the Labyrinth. The Minotaur was placed at its center and sacrifices were made to it.

In the same way that early European Man acted out the hunt and dressed as a horned animal, so it was until relatively recent times with the American Indians. The Penobscot Indians would wear deer masks. The Mandan Indians, before hunting buffalo, would perform a ritual dance dressed in buffalo heads and skins.

Although the god of the Old Religion was thought of as horned he certainly did not have a forked, or pointed tail. Yet the Christian Devil is usually depicted as having horns and tail and, as we have seen, the Old God was equated with this figure. The Christian chroniclers would automatically write the word "Devil" or "Satan" in the court records when the witch on trial used the word "God". In illustrations to the early books witches are shown worshipping a figure not only with horns and a tail but frequently with bat-wings as well.

Popular novelists have played on this misrepresentation. Dennis Wheatley, an English writer, has written a number of Black Magic novels in which a Christian Devil deity is worshipped by a group that he labels "witches": "Until the candles had been lit, the pale violet halo which emanated from the figure had been enough to show that it was human and the face undoubtedly black. But, as they watched, it changed to a greyish color, and something was happening to the formation of the head.

'It is the Goat of Mendes, Rex!' whispered the

Duke. 'My God! this is horrible!' And even as he spoke, the manifestation took on a clearer shape; the hands, held forward almost in an attitude of prayer but turned downward, became transformed into two great cloven hoofs. Above rose the monstrous bearded head of a gigantic goat, appearing to be at least three times the size of any other which they had ever seen. The two slit-eyes, slanting inwards and down, gave out a red, baleful light. Long pointed ears cocked upwards from the sides of the shaggy head, and from the bald, horrible unnatural bony skull, which was caught by the light of the candles, four enormous curved horns spread out—sideways and up."*

That there are groups of people who do believe in such a devil, and worship him as a personification of evil, is indesputable. But these people are *not* witches. To go back to the *Rosemary's Baby* setting, they are incorrectly called witches by authors who are ignorant. They are actually Satanists.

Perhaps the best known group of Satanists was the notorious eighteenth century group led by Sir Francis Dashwood and popularly known as the Hell-Fire Club. They called themselves The Friars of St. Francis of Wycombe, but the "Hell-Fire Club" label was much more appropriate. The young nobleman, Sir Francis, had been through a period of extreme piety and dedication to the

The Devil Rides Out, London, 1934

Roman Catholic Church. It was the result of witnessing, as he thought, a visitation by an angel. When he later learned that the "angel" had been his private tutor dressed in his night-shirt, and that his resultant religiousness was making him the laughing stock of Regency London, he swore to avenge the trickery.

Sir Francis had inherited a considerable fortune from his father and he put it to work in the construction of a suitable meeting place for his followers. Basing his group on Jesus and the Apostles he took to himself twelve of the young rakes of the time. He called himself Jesus and each member went by the name of an Apostle. He bought a ruined Medieval abbey on the bank of the Thames, and had it restored complete with stained glass windows showing himself and his followers engaged in various sexual acts. The Abbey had originally been built in 1160 and was called Medmenham. They all dressed in monk's robes and assumed a pose of great piety—but dedicated to the Devil and all forms of evil. Their ceremonies were parodies of Catholic ones and it is certain that they performed the Black Mass.

Sir Francis would have numbers of prostitutes on hand at the abbey for the entertainment of his followers after the rituals. These women he would have dressed as nuns. Since the members were all men of position, not without influence at Court, there was little that could be done about this upper-class sacrilege. The club flourished for many years only collapsing on the eventual death of Sir Francis himself, in 1781. The membership varied over the years as the original followers either died or dropped out for some reason, and their places were taken by others. Lord Bute was once a member, as was George Selwyn, Thomas Potter (son of the Archbishop of Canterbury), the Earl of Sandwich and even, for a brief period, Benjamin Franklin.

There is a story told—almost certainly true—of the occasion when Sir Francis allowed a certain priest to use the grounds attached to his home for a children's outing. The children were running about, in and out the decorative hedges and by the fountains, having a wonderful time. The priest went to thank Sir Francis for being such a benefactor. Sir Francis merely beckoned the priest to follow him, and led the way up the stairs to the top of a tower overlooking the gardens below. To his horror the priest saw that the low, beautifully-kept hedges, around which the young children frolicked, were actually skilfully laid out to represent the outline of a naked woman. As the priest looked on, stunned, Sir Francis pressed a switch and the three fountains, strategically placed, gushed forth—the two upper ones, in the breasts, with a white liquid, and the lower one, from a triangle of shrubbery, with a yellow liquid. This was indeed typical of the elaborate jokes arranged by Sir Francis.

Over the entrance to the abbey was an inscription which was the only law of the group. It was taken from Rabelais and was, simply, "Do What Thou Wilt". The "monks" needed no urging, they were able to satisfy their every desire, no matter how bizarre. This same motto was taken by a latter-day Franciscan, Aleister Crowley. "Do What Thou Wilt Shall Be The Whole of The Law", was to become the basic tenet of his own religion.

Born in England in 1875, into a well-to-do but rigidly religious family, Crowley rebelled against his parents at a very early age. His father was actually a Plymouth Brethren minister. Such was young Aleister's rebellion against the Victorian sanctimoniousness that his mother declared him to be the Great Beast, whose number is 666, from thb Book of Revelations. Aleister's fancy was captured by such a description and for the rest of his life played out the role to the full. He was fascinated by magic and had soon gathered together a collection of old books on the subject. He learned Hebrew in order to study the Kabala. When the opportunity arose he joined the famous Order of the Golden Dawn and rapidly rose to its upper ranks. Among its members were W. B. Yeats and Israel Regardie. Another member was S.L. MacGregor-Mathers. Mathers one day discovered an ancient magical manuscript (known as a *grimoire*) dating from the fifteenth century. It was titled *The Book of Sacred Magic of Abra-Melin the Mage*. A *mage* is a magician; a ceremonial magic practitioner. Mathers translated the manuscript from its original Hebrew and Crowley decided to put it to the test.

If Crowley had been able to keep his attention to magic exclusively for a long period of time, there is no knowing what he might have accomplished. However the *Abra-Melin* involved seclusion and complete sexual abstinence for a period prior to the magic ritual. If there was one thing that Crowley had a weakness for besides magic, it was sex. Complete abstinence was therefore not to his liking. He finally broke his seclusion before completing the ritual.

His life was filled with magical practises and sex rites. He lived with various women at different times, usually wealthy ones. Once he had used up all their money he would drop them and move on. At one point in his life he came into contact with witchcraft (This is certain because there is, in Gerald Gardner's collection on the Isle of Man, a copy of a Book of Shadows written entirely in Crowley's handwriting). Obviously he found the Craft too tame for his tastes because he did not remain in it. After a great deal of searching he reached the conclusion that the only way to have a religion that was ideally suited to him was to start one himself.

This he did, and it is not surprising to find that it was a more or less equal mixture of magic and sex. He purchased an old stone building on the island of Sicily, near the village of Cefalu.

This he called his Abbey of Thelema. He lived there with his two women, one known as his "Scarlet Woman," or "Whore of the Great Beast", the other known simply as "Cyprus". A painter of sorts he decorated the walls and ceiling of the abbey with wild, orgiastic scenes; the floor with magic circles and symbols. He had some years earlier dictated a *Book of Law* for his religion to his woman/wife of the time, Rose Kelly, sister of Sir Gerald Kelly. It was dictated in Cairo and he was, supposedly, in a trance as he dictated, his Guardian Angel—or Demon—speaking through him.

People came from as far away as America to visit Crowley at his Abbey at Cefalu. There they might well have witnessed such a ritual as Crowley's wife copulating with a goat, the goat being sacrificed at the moment of orgasm. This was supposed to release a tremendous magical power (which it might well have done) but what he attempted to do with that power, how he tried to harness it, is not recorded. Eventually his rituals led to the death of one of his followers, Raoul Loveday—through drinking the blood of a sacrificed cat—and he was ordered out of the country. He finally died, in December 1947, in England. At his funeral a friend read his *Hymn to Pan*, from one of his rituals. Typically enough the local press reported that a Black Mass had been performed at the funeral, but this was not the case. His religion, generally labelled "Crowleyanity", is still followed by some today.

The present-day equivalent of Sir Francis Dashwood and Aleister Crowley is a man named Anton Lavey. Lavey's name would crop up from time to time in local newspapers in the San Francisco area. He was an actor for a while, then he was with a circus. One day he hit on the idea of forming a church for Satanists. He has a house on California Street, San Francisco, and it was here that he established The First Satanic Church of the United States. To fit the part he shaved his head, grew a pointed beard, took to wearing what has been described as "a balaclava with horns", and took to spelling his name "LaVey". In no time at all he had a very large following. Many people, it seemed, were longing to show their disdain for the organized Church of today. Almost certainly sixty to eighty per cent of these self-styled Satanists had no real belief in the Devil, or wish to pay him homage. They joined for "kicks". They joined because it was the "IN" thing to do. Even Lavey himself was more interested in the commercial side of his "church". In an interview with *Fate* magazine (September 1967) he said that each potential follower is subjected to a special financial analysis. The less affluent "simply are asked not to return".

As he describes it "calling it a church enabled me to follow the magic formula of nine parts outrage to one part social respectability that is needed for success." The creed of this Church of

Satan urges full indulgence in the Seven Deadly Sins. Already a Satanic marriage has taken place. Not quite up to the standard of Rosemary's copulation with the Devil, it did however get full press coverage. A New York Republican of some note was somewhat surprised to find that his daughter, Judith Case, was the bride. The groom was an out-of-work writer named John Raymond. As described in the press the couple were joined in unholy matrimony, before "an altar on which lay a naked woman". In actual fact the woman was three-quarters covered by an imitation leopard skin, and was laying on the mantle above the fireplace in the Lavey living-room, where the ceremony was conducted.

Initiation into the Church of Satan involves filling out a questionaire and paying a fee of $13.00. In return you will receive "*Lifetime* membership in the Church of Satan . . . A suitably inscribed membership card . . . Complete instructions for performing *authentic* Satanic rituals . . . A list of other members . . . Bimonthly reading lists . . ."

One such reading list contains such titles as *The Morning of the Magicians* (Pauwels and Bergier), *The Black Arts* (Cavendish), *The Philosophy of Nietzsche* (ed. Clive), and *The New Intellectual* (Rand).

You can, of course, send for such accessories as an "18 inch Baphomet symbol . . . on heavy-guage masonite" (just $13.00) and "the first recording in history of an authentic Satanic Ceremony," a stereo long-playing record entitled *The Satanic Mass*, for $5.00.

Tremendous interest has been taken in Lavey's venture, to the point where branches of the church are being formed across the country. Lavey had collected a number of books on magic, both black and ceremonial. Borrowing heavily from these he drew up his own ceremonies and eventually wrote a Satanic Bible. In this he gives the "Nine Satanic Statements". They include such platitudes as "Satan represents indulgence, instead of abstinence! Satan represents all of the so-called sins, as they all lead to physical, mental, or emotional gratification!" and the final (perhaps true?) "Satan has been the best friend the Church has ever had, as he has kept it in business all these years!"

In the various chapters that follow Lavey expands on the ways of the good Satanist. There is even a chapter on human sacrifice, though it is noteworthy that he ends it saying "You have every right to (*symbolically*)* destroy . . ." Obviously he realizes that however much fun it is to play at Satanism he must still stay within the law. He falls far short of Aleister Crowley. Although Crowley did not call himself a Satanist he was actually far more of one than Lavey could ever be. Crowley lived the part, while Lavey acts it.

*author's italics

Wood Carving of Witch from Gypsy Caravan—1850.

CHAPTER 11
THE WITCH ALONE

Do witches only exist in groups or covens? What of individual witches? One way to find the answers to these questions, which are often asked, is to make the comparison between witchcraft *as a religion*, and any other religion. For example, can a person be a Christian without belonging to a church; without attending the services of the Christian faith? He can certainly *live his life* according to the Christian teachings, yes. He can love his neighbor, turn the other cheek, thank God for what he has, and do all those things expected of "a good Christian". But most important to, for example, the Catholic faith, are the sacraments. He can hardly celebrate a Mass by himself, for the priest alone can consecrate the elements of the Mass. As a Catholic he would be expected to go to Mass on Sundays, have his children baptized and instructed in the faith, go to confession, say the rosary, marry within the church. A baptism and a later confirmation are two very important elements in Christianity. As with Christianity (or Judaism, Shinto, Islam) so with witchcraft, for there is the Initiation (and, in the case of a child, a later confirmation). So you *may* follow the religion of witchcraft alone, but that in itself does not make you a witch *per se*.

In the past there have been many who have been referred to as witches and who, in many aspects, were such without having been initiated and belonging to a coven (as with the person we have just been discussing, "living the life of" a Christian). They may well, in the old days, have even been referred to as *Wica*—remembering that *wica* means, literally, "wise one". There were almost certainly many cases where a man or woman was looked upon in this capacity, was consulted for medicines, charms, advice, yet did not belong to a coven. Perhaps because there was no coven within reach. In many parts of Europe, after the Persecutions had died down, there must have been many individuals cut-off from their covens or, never having belonged, unable to establish initial contact. These are the types who became "the witch alone".

Exactly what can such an individual do? There are many things for there is magic which can be practised alone. However one important thing about practising magic in a coven is that this gives a built-in safety factor. The group as a whole must be in complete agreement as to what is going to be done. Therefore if one member of the coven should, for example, be rather quick-tempered and should be so highly incensed over something that she should want to "get back at" someone who had done her wrong, then the coven as a whole would have to be all equally incensed, which is unlikely to happen. In a state of excitement, particularly of anger, you could do great harm without fully realising the consequences of what you were doing. The other coven members, therefore, act as a balancing agent—the High Priestess especially—and see that however angry you are, nothing would be done to harm anyone.

The witch working alone does not have this restraining influence, and so is in the position of having to rigidly control her emotions herself, lest she do something which, in returning threefold, would be disastrous for her. If she restricts herself to healing, for example, she should have no problem.

Everyone is familiar, if only from fiction, with the wax figure stuck with pins. Such a figure is typical of sympathetic magic and is actually one of the oldest forms of it. The same basic principles —sticking in pins to injure the victim—can be applied to work good. For example, a man may be suffering from terrible back-ache. The witch could take some wax, or clay, and fashion a figure to represent the man. It would not have to be an exact likeness, in fact it could be quite a crude "gingerbread-man" type figure. But all the while it was being moulded she would keep a clear picture of the man in her mind. If she had a photograph of him which she could lay beside her on which to concentrate, all the better. When the figure was finished then she would stick three or four pins in its back—or wherever the pain happened to be. When sticking in the pins she would try *not* to think of the pain he was experiencing, for at this point she would be merely

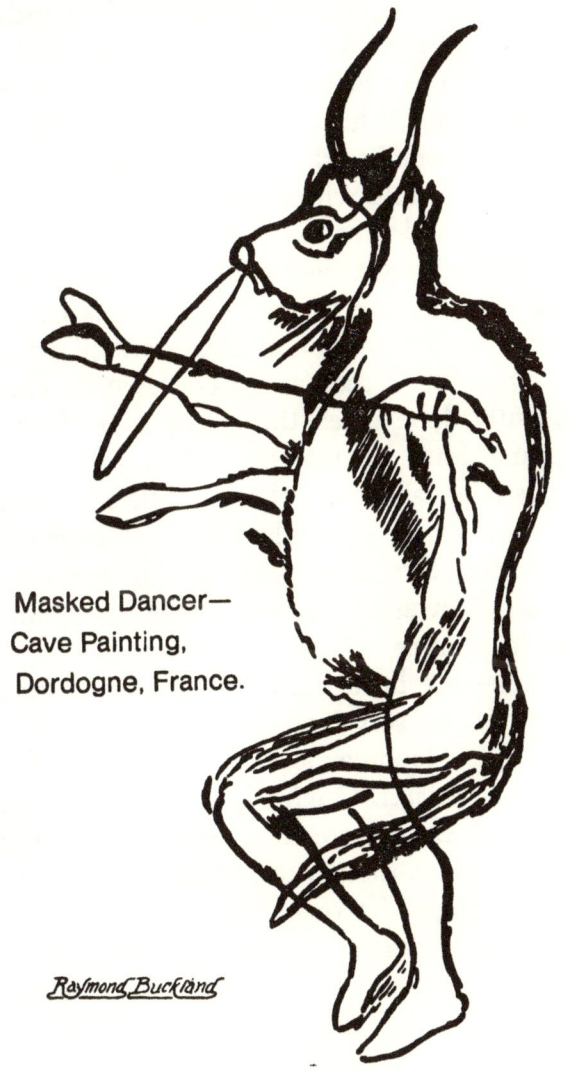

Masked Dancer—
Cave Painting,
Dordogne, France.

placing them preparatory to doing the healing.

The next step would be to actually name the figure for the recipient. This would be done by sprinkling and censing it and by saying the words to the effect, "Here lies John Doe, who seeks relief from pain. All that I do to him here is done also to his person". The witch would then concentrate as hard as she could on the man, seeing him as being fit and well, without the back-ache. One by one she would then draw out the pins thinking, and perhaps even saying words to the effect, that she was drawing the pain out of his body.

Another, similar, ritual is often performed using a cloth figure rather than a wax or clay one. This is frequently done when the person is suffering from some form of infection. The figure, or *poppet* as it is called, can then be filled with an herb suitable for the particular healing to be done. For example, camomile is good for reducing swellings; knapweed for ulcers; fennel for asthma and also for cramps.

An interesting little book full of old charms and cures of the sort used by many lone "wise ones" is J.G. Hohman's *Pow-wows*, subtitled *the long lost friend*. Originally published at the beginning of the nineteenth century it is still selling well today, though the efficacy of some of its recipes might be open to question. *Ozark Superstitions* is another most interesting book containing a variety of cures, charms, beliefs, etc., held by the people of that area and collected by Vance Randolph. One of the items is a love-potion used in north-western Arkansas. It is made from the web of a wild gander's foot, dried and reduced to powder. It is claimed that a pinch of this in a girl's drink will guarantee her falling in love with you and remaining forever faithful. Should a girl wish to bring her boyfriend to see her she has only to throw salt on the fire for seven consecutive mornings and he will be irresistably drawn to her.

A way to cure boils is to rub a greasy string on a rusty nail and then throw the nail far away, where it cannot be found. Take the string and hang it inside the front door of your house. At least seven times a day touch the boil with the string and the boil will gradually disappear. There are an incredible number of such cures available if you have the patience to collect them.

John Baptista Porta's book *Natural Magick*, published in 1658, contains a wonderful miscellany of "physicks". An example is his "excellent remedy . . . to fasten teeth". As he says, it "strengthens and fasteneth them: yea, if they are eaten away, it filleth them with flesh, and new clothes them".

"Take therefore three handfuls of sage, nettles, rosemary, mallows, and the rind of the roots of walnut; wash them well, and beat them: also, as much of the flowers of sage, rosemary, olive and plantaine leaves; two handfuls of hypocistic, horehound, and the tops of bramble; one pound of the flower of mirtle; half a pound of the seed; two handfuls of rosebuds, with their stalks; two drachms of saunders, coriander prepared, and citron-pill: three drachms of cinnamon in powder; ten of cypress nuts; five green pineapples; two drachms of bole-armenick and mastick. Powder them all, and infuse them in sharp black wine, put them into an alembick*, and fill them with a gentle fire: then boil the distilled water, with two ounces of allome till it be dissolved, in a vessel cloth-stopped. When you would use it, suck up some of the water, and stir it up and down in your mouth until it turn to froth: then spit it out, and rub your teeth with a linen-cloth. It will perform what I have promised: for it fasteneth the teeth, and restoreth the gums that are eroded"!

How much more simple his formula for immunity to the Plague: "Gather Ivy-berries in May, and wild poppies before the sun rise, lest they open; in April gather goat's rue: dry them in the shade, and make them into powder. One drachm of it being drunk in wine is excellent against infectious diseases."

One whole section of Porta's book is dedicated to "Beautifying Women" and includes such headings as "To dye the hair yellow, . . .red, . . . black; to make hair curl; to make the face white; to make the face very soft; to take wrinkles from the body; to correct the ill scent of the armpits;

*apparatus formerly used in distilling.

how the matrix over-widened in childbirth may be made narrower; A woman deflowered made a virgin again," and many other gems!

* * *

A more advanced "witch alone" might have access to some book of magic such as the rare *Book of Sacred Magic of Abra-Melin the Mage* (on which Aleister Crowley based much of his magic). From this, apart from the more involved details of ceremonial magic comprising the main body of the book, she might get such details as how to "know secrets, and especially those of any person; to transform animals into men, and men into animals; to excite tempests; to walk and operate in and under water; to fly in the air and go wherever one may wish; to open every kind of lock without a key, and without noise; for all kinds of affection and love."

The basis of this magic is a series of Kabalistic squares of letters, which are actually so many pentacles and in which the names employed are the real factors operating. For example the "Magic Square" to heal sea-sickness is given as shown on page 174.

Eleos and *hals* mean "the sea from its saltness". *Elos* means "calm, still water".

This Magic Square should be written on parchment and then fastened to the forehead of the sick person. Sometimes the letters are written in one of the "Magical Alphabets" such as *Celestial Writing, Theban, Passing the River,* or *Angelic.*

*Although the squares themselves look simple they are deceptively so, for it is not just a matter of drawing lines and filling in with odd letters. In fact the preparation is such that in the *Abra-Melin* the first two thirds of the book tells in detail how to prepare yourself to make the squares. As Margaret Bruce, a recognized expert on Ceremonial Magic, once told me, "The effect of following the instructions is to produce that state of mental and physical tension which is an essential if any act of Magick is to have results. The interesting feature of the Abra-Melin squares is that they contain letters rather than (the more often encountered) numbers, and that these letters form words and names, often of a palindromic nature."

Another item frequently dealt with by an individual witch or magician is the talisman. Talismans are of many types, dependant upon the purpose for which they are desired. You can have a talisman for love, or one for luck in a particular endeavor. Again to quote Margaret Bruce, "Many people seem to think that a talisman or amulet should protect one from all harm, attract unlimited wealth, and make one beloved of the world at large. Such an idea is superstition of the worst possible kind and betrays a lack of understanding of the very nature of Magick and talis-

*See page 174.

mans . . . *The people who think that Magick should enable them to go through life without any personal effort are morally and emotionally immature, and thus incapable of making Magick work in any case."*

Ideally a talisman should be made by the actual person who is to use it. It should be made in the appropriate hour. In other words, a talisman for love would be made on a Friday, since that is the day governed by Venus, and at the time of day when the Sun is in Libra or Taurus and the Moon is trine to Venus. The metal of the talisman should be the metal of Venus—copper. The actual design engraved on it, known as a *sigil*, is a traditional one found in any of the better-known grimoires, such as *The Key of Solomon the King, The Heptameron, The Red Tree of Gana,* or *The Almadel.*

Once the talisman is made it must be kept "alive". This is done through a simple ritual once a month, usually at a particular phase of the moon, when the talisman is, in effect, rejuvenated.

So it is possible, in effect, to be a witch alone—so far as the magical side of witchcraft goes. But such a person could not celebrate the Festivals alone; could not do the rituals of Esbat and Sabbat; could not even know the names of the gods. Since witchcraft is *first and foremost* a religion such an individual would not be recognized by true, initiated, coven witches.

E	L	E	O	S
L	A	B	I	O
E	B	I	B	E
O	I	B	A	L
S	O	E	L	E

Magic Square from
The Book of Sacred Magic
of Abra-Melin The Mage (1485)

CHAPTER 12
"LET'S ALL CAST SPELLS!"

At the very beginning of this book I mentioned the tremendous interest in the occult found everywhere today. Everyone, it seems, is an overnight expert on the tarot, the I-Ching, astrology, palmistry. It is the IN thing. It is also the IN thing to be a witch, and all over the country are popping-up pseudo witches and spurious covens. Unfortunately (for the true witch) it is easy for anyone to claim to be of the Craft. They can spout the most outlandish drivel and no one, apparently, can prove them wrong. We suddenly find a woman touring the country getting herself proclaimed the "Official Witch" of wherever. Apparently she collects cities like scalps. When asked, on television recently, what her duties were as such an "official witch" she lamely replied that she was "in an advisory capacity"! We trust there is no retaining fee involved.

Another would-be witch, a self-confessed homosexual, announces that he is going to form "The Church of the Gay Witch"! A "gay witch" would be an absolute contradiction in terms. Being a religion of nature the witch is very much heterosexual; there must be male and female, equal numbers of each, in a coven. Apparently this particular person found that he was a witch when another self-styled witch met him, looked hard at him and said, "Greetings, fellow witch!" *Ergo* he *was* a witch and has considered himself one ever since.

A young magazine photographer not so long ago came to visit my museum and take pictures. He brought with him a young lady who not only "knew" she was a witch—and announced the fact to everyone she met—but even gave her name the prefix "witch". It was interesting that many of the witchcraft items in the museum she completely failed to recognise. Her excuse? "Well we have sort of dropped the—er—religious side of it. We just get together for the big festivals." When asked what she did at, for example, Hallowe'en she did not seem too sure but finally decided they did a "sort of rejuvenating ritual. We sort of re-charge ourselves".

All of these so-called witches invariably claim ancestors who had been burned at the stake. Some even claim an ancestor who was *burned* at Salem—where there was nothing but hangings! A young man in Massachusetts says "Three of my great-great-grandfathers were burned to death as witches. I believe witchcraft is hereditary; I've always known I would become a warlock."

It is not uncommon to hear such a remark as "I can trace my ancestors back to a famous witch of the sixteenth century." Yet when I have challenged such a statement the speaker has had difficulty in producing documentary proof even back to his (or her) grandparents! The pattern seems to be that they come across mention of a witch trial where someone with a name the same as theirs, or perhaps just similar, was charged with witchcraft. Immediately they adopt an ancestor!

What harm is there in all this? Basically none whatsoever, for the only person they are really fooling is themselves. Most witches—true witches—prefer to keep in the background. If the subject of witchcraft comes up in conversation they are more than likely to change the subject. Most of the self-styled witches eventually hang themselves, metaphorically speaking of course. They are in the public eye for a while and then the novelty wears off. Either that or they are so obviously unversed in their subject that they fall from favor. The more colorful ones can actually do witchcraft a favor for they tend to attract the "nuts" to themselves, thus keeping them from the true Craft.

It is amusing to see how some contradict themselves or make statements so obviously incorrect that they could never in a million years be real witches. However the only ones who really do no good whatsoever to the Craft are those such as "Maria" (who, incidentally, claims to "trace her ancestry to the pre-Inquisition, and who had three of her ancestors burned at the stake"), who spends all her time cursing the Catholic Church. She claims to practise the Black Mass (all by herself?) and apparently goes to St. Patrick's Cathedral, New York, every Sunday for the express purpose of obtaining the Eucharist. She smuggles it home and then sits stabbing it, in the name of her murdered ancestors! Gerald Gardner, in *The Meaning of Witchcraft*, says "To a Roman Catholic who believes in Transubstantiation, that is that the bread and wine of the Mass are literally changed into the flesh and blood of Christ, a ceremonial insult to the Host would be the most awful blasphemy; *but witches do not believe this, so it would simply be absurd to them to try to insult a piece of bread.*" Gardner, of course, was not the first to point this out. In fact he mentions that Eliphas Levi, the famous French occultist—who also happened to be a Catholic—had said that the first condition of success in black magic was to be prepared to profane the cultus in which you *believed*.

* * *

Many who claim to be witches—the "Official Witch of Everytown", for instance—know perfectly well themselves whether or not they are of the Craft. These are the ones who are labelled, by true witches, as "Commercial Witches". They are in the game for fame and fortune—as much as they can get of either, preferably both. But there are many who honestly do believe themselves to be witches and are not especially seeking recognition for themselves in the capacity. They might have read somewhere, or heard from one of the aforementioned, that "the seventh child of a seventh child is a witch". Or perhaps that "anyone born on Hallowe'en is a witch". Some even believe that the ability, or even just the desire, to read tea-leaves automatically enrolls them. But with these people witches have no quarrel, for they are just misinformed. They may even be potential Craft members. If they like to think of themselves as already witches it does not matter. They may have the interest, they might also have some ability. Witches do not proselytize for they believe that those meant for the Craft will find it.

There are those who know they are not witches, who wish to be witches, but can get no contact with the Craft. The problem is, what can they do? Many of them decide that imitation is the sincerest form of flattery. They read such worthwhile books as those of Gardner, Murray and Lethbridge. From these they put together rituals of their own, following the feelings of the Craft as closely as they can. They invariably feel strongly towards the old gods of the Craft and, though they do not know their names, worship them in their own way. Since, as has been mentioned, it is more important to speak from the heart than it is to adhere to a set form of words, then this type of freeflowing would-be witchcraft is not to be discouraged.

There is a group of teenagers in one area, many of whom attend the same high school. They are all very well read on the subject of witchcraft and, like so many other people, from reading Gardner and Murray especially, have developed a tremendous feeling for the Craft. They were unable to locate a coven—"We found one or two people who claimed to be witches but soon found that they knew even less than we did," they told me—so they finally decided to start their own. They wrote some truly beautiful rituals, drawing on Sir James Frazer and Robert Graves, and met together regularly to worship. Realising that at their age meeting together skyclad would not be the best of plans they decided to wear loose-fitting robes.

Recently this group did come into contact with a coven. The coven is now watching over them and guiding them on Craft lines. Eventually they will all be initiated and will become a true coven. Through their careful research in the construction of their original rites they will find the transition a very easy and natural one. Groups such as theirs, indeed individuals such as them, are to be encouraged and are doubly welcomed into the Craft when they eventually find it. It is certainly better all round that they be doing something positive than just sitting bemoaning the fact that they cannot find what they seek.

Almost the reverse side of the coin is seen in a group located not far from these youngsters. This group is older, if only in years. They too had been fascinated by the Craft. However, with very little searching for a coven they decided to form their own. They wrote their rituals, basing them mainly on the rituals of ceremonial magic. Where they seriously erred, and where they earned the displeasure of many true covens who later heard of them, was that they then set out to proselytize. They contacted others and set about establishing other covens, using their own home-made rituals, but *passing them on as the time-honored traditional rites of the Wica*. They would "initiate" High Priestesses by mail—without the trouble of first passing through the lower degrees—and send out copies, frequently sadly incomplete, of their "Book of Shadows". One small point in their favor, though it is possible that they just overlooked an opportunity, is that they did not charge any fee for their "initiations". In the Craft there is *never* a charge, for an initiation or for anything done in the Circle. This is as it should be. If ever a person, seeking the Craft, is told that someone will take them into it for a fee . . .it will not be the Craft he is entering.

* * *

Witches believe in a power coming from the human body, as was shown in Chapter 9. But this is a power which is inherent in *everyone*, not only witches. As has been shown witches have ways of drawing off this power very strongly, and directing it. But there are individuals who have it very strongly quite naturally. A well-known example would be Jean Dixon, the Washington, D.C., realtor. Mrs. Dixon is a Roman Catholic, yet she can see into a crystal ball and predicts the future. Obviously she is not a witch (though, equally obviously, she would have been executed as one in the Middle Ages). There are other people who are just as obviously not witches but who can use their powers as Mrs. Dixon can. E.S.P. (extra-sensory perception) is a very common example of the power. Many people have experienced E.S.P. at work yet they are not witches.

To reverse the above statement, then, it can be seen that just because someone can use a crystal ball, or demonstrate E.S.P., this is not proof that she is a witch. So for someone to say, in effect, "I have the ability to do this, that and the other—*ergo* I am a witch!" is complete nonsense. The vast majority of witches do not claim to be witches and in fact frequently claim *not* to be witches. I say "the vast majority" because there are one or two true witches who have been chosen, perhaps because of their position of their personality or knowledge, to do a certain amount (not excessive) of public relations work. Gerald Gardner was the first of these. They are invariably of the priesthood of the Craft and what they do is to see that from time to time worthwhile exposure of witchcraft is given. By "worthwhile exposure" I mean articles, books, lectures or the like that will help straighten the popular misconceptions on the Wica. It is my sincere hope that *this* book is one such.

CHAPTER 13

WAYS OF WITCHCRAFT

In the preceding chapters we have looked at the ways of witchcraft from the points of view of the Church and of the witches themselves. We have seen that the majority of popular conceptions of witchcraft are actually *mis*conceptions. The reason is ably summed up by Pennethorne Hughes when he draws a parallel with Nazi Germany and the Jews: "the record of witchcraft is that set down by its enemies. It is as though, in a world conquered by the Third Reich, all Jewish tradition and history had been destroyed—together with the Bible and all the Jews themselves—so that later generations knew of Jews only as portrayed by the men of Nuremberg."

For centuries, from the beginning of Christianity, the New Religion and the Old actually existed side by side. It was usually a peaceful coexistence, so far as the people were concerned. But the New Religion was not happy at that. It had to be the *only* religion. So, as we have seen, there were the various papal bulls against the Wica, culminating in Innocent VIII's widely distributed "Hammer" of the Witches.

Much worse, by far, than the supposed crimes of the witches themselves were the actual crimes of the witch-hunters. Those men who made a living from seeking-out witches. Frequently they chose the youngest, prettiest women, that they might be stripped and searched. Tortures, when applied,—whether legally or not—were of the most terrible. Evidence of the type never normally acceptable in court was found quite acceptable in witch trials.

Ronald Seth's *Children Against Witches* deals with some of this normally unacceptable evidence. Studying various English trials of the fifteenth, sixteenth and early seventeenth centuries he shows how many people were hung on the charge of witchcraft solely on the evidence of children, some as young as six years old.

Confessions to the whole gammut of professed witchcraft were not uncommon. Podmore (*Modern Spiritualism*) comments on this: "The confessions, as is notorious, were for the most part extracted under torture, or by lying promises of release. In England, where torture was not countenanced by the law, the ingenuity of Matthew Hopkins and other professional witch-finders would generally devise some equally efficient substitute, such as gradual starvation, enforced sleeplessness, or the maintenance for hours of a constrained and painful posture. But apart from these extorted confessions. there is evidence that in some cases the accused persons were actually driven by the accumulation of testimony against them, by the pressure of public opinion, and the singular circumstances in which they were placed, to believe and confess that they were witches indeed. Some of the women in Salem who had pleaded guilty to witchcraft explained afterwards, when the persecution had died down and they were released, that they had been 'consternated and affrighted even out of their reason' to confess that of which they were innocent. And there were not a few persons who voluntarily confessed to the practise of witchcraft, nocturnal rides, compacts with the devil, and all the rest of it."

Most of the evidence presented by the supposed victims of the witch's *maleficia* was of a ridiculous nature. A farmer's cow ran dry or his horse stumbled. His cart lost a wheel or his child was sick. All this would be blamed on the one accused of witchcraft. Frequently the incidents referred to had occurred five, ten, or even twenty years before. It was a great way to settle old debts. It was also a great way, as was shown with the Berwick Witches, to make a political move.

Charles Godfrey Leland, in his *Aradia, the Gospel of the Witches*, dealt with the witchcraft of Italy as reported to him, at the end of the nineteenth century, by a woman claiming to be a witch. She delivered to him a copy of a gospel (*vangelo*) which is obviously of some antiquity, possibly dating from the Middle Ages. As Lethbridge points out, it does suffer from a certain amount of political propoganda from the time when "the peasant populations of western Europe had found that Church and State were both oppressors." But it is still of considerable value. It mentions much that has since been brought to light by the witches themselves—the nakedness at the rites, the monthly meetings at the full of the moon, the worship of the gods.

Margaret Murray, we have seen, was chiefly responsible for this new look at witchcraft. Her hypothesis that witchcraft was in reality the maligned descendant of an ancient nature-religion started many scholars on the trail which led back to early Man's animistic beliefs. Professor E.O. James, in *Prehistoric Religion* and *Ancient Gods*, has brought forth much evidence to support Murray's theories, particularly where the Mother Goddess is concerned. Brian Branston, in *The Lost Gods of England*, reconstructs the pantheon of the Anglo-Saxons and does much to bring into perspective the thinking of these early people where religion is concerned.

Witchcraft was, and is, a religion which evolved slowly and naturally as Man himself evolved. For this reason it is a religion easily understood and readily acceptable by the majority of people. With the repeal of the old laws against witchcraft, and with the groundwork done by Murray *et al*, present-day witches were finally able to come forward and present their side of the picture. Gerald Gardner was the first, and probably the best, such spokesman.

So the true picture is slowly emerging, even though the effect of centuries of misrepresentation lingers. As we saw at the beginning of this book such stories as *Rosemary's Baby* perpetrate the incorrect ideas. Rosemary's neighbors, we can see now, were Satanists and a far cry from followers of the Old Religion. The inference of witchcraft with the Sharon Tate murders was of the same old Satanic/ritual-sacrifice type.

Will witchcraft ever become a "great power" in

the world? I think not. Almost certainly it will eventually be accepted for what it is, despite the Marias, the Levins, the Wheatleys and others of that ilk. I do not think it will ever be a religion comparable, in influence, to Roman Catholicism, for example. I do not think it would ever want to be. Witchcraft is obviously not the religion for everybody. Yet, with the present dissatisfaction with other more orthodox religions, it is obviously the answer for many who are presently "seeking".

From this you might say "Right! I've decided it is for me. Where do I go from here?" As I said in Chapter 8 should you feel genuinely interested you are certainly welcome to write to me. This is *not* to say that I will initiate you, or even bring you into contact with a coven, but I am always happy to discuss witchcraft and to answer, so far as I am able, any questions on the subject. But before anyone finally makes up their mind I would strongly recommend that they read just as much as possible on the subject. A great deal has been written, much of it nonsense. But there *are* worthwhile books, and I have included a bibliography at the end of this volume for those who would like to read further. Some of the books may not be easy to find. Yet I feel they are well worth searching for.

Beware the young lady who boldly proclaims, for no apparent reason, "I am a witch!" This is not to say that she definitely is *not* one — but the odds are certainly against her. Beware newspaper advertisements announcing "Courses in witchcraft" or suggesting that there is an opening in a coven. Witches very definitely do not advertise. Beware especially, the promise to have you initiated for a fee. After all, you wouldn't consider paying a large sum to be baptized into a Christian religion. Why, then, pay to become a pagan?

It is frequently suggested that, because of the connotations of evil associated with witchcraft in the popular mind, witches should change their name. There are two thoughts on this. One is, why should we? Just because many people think of witchcraft as being evil this does not make it so. "Witch" comes from *wica,* meaning "wise". Far better, surely, to educate the ignorant to the correct interpretation than to hide under another name.

The other thought is a somewhat defeatist one. Supposing witches *did* change their name. Suppose they called themselves, say, "The Naturites". How long before someone would say, "Yes, they call themselves 'Naturites' but they're not really, you know. They're really witches!" So change the name again—and again. And keep running.

No. Better to stay the true name, and correct the misconceptions. With the many latter-day "witches", particularly in the drug scene, a number of the Craft do tend to use the original "Wica" rather than the word "witch" but this, in effect, is a part of correcting.

"Wica" or "witch", we are what we are. I hope that this book has helped, if only a little, in showing what that is.

BIBLIOGRAPHY

BAROJA, J.C.—*The World of Witches.* London, 1964
BRACELIN, J.—*Gerald Gardner: Witch.* London, n.d.
BRANSTON, Brian—*The Lost Gods of England.* London 1957
BURLAND, C.A.—*The Magical Arts.* New York, 1966
BURR, G.L. (Ed.)—*Narratives of the Witchcraft Cases 1648-1706.* New York, 1914
BUCKLAND, Raymond—*Witchcraft From the Inside.* Minn. 1970
—*A Pocket Guide to the Supernatural.* New York. 1969
FRAZER, Sir James—*The Golden Bough.* New York, 1935
GARDNER, Gerald—*High Magic's Aid.* London. 1949
—*Witchcraft Today.* London, 1954
—*The Meaning of Witchcraft.* London, 1959
GLASS, Justine—*Witchcraft, the Sixth Sense and Us.* London, 1965
GRAVES, Robert—*The White Goddess.* New York, 1966
HILL, D & WILLIAMS, P—*The Supernatural.* London, 1965
HOLE, Christina—*Witchcraft in England.* London, 1945

HUGHES, Pennethorne—*Witchcraft*. London, 1952
JAMES, E.O.—*Ancient Gods*. London, 1960
KITTERIDGE, G.L.—*Witchcraft in Old and New England*. Mass. 1929
LELAND, C.G.—*Aradia, Gospel of the Witches*. London, 1899
LETHBRIDGE, T.C.—*Witches*. London, 1962
MICHELET, Jules—*Satanism and Witchcraft*. New York, 1939
MURRAY, Margaret A.—*The Witch Cult in Western Europe*. London, 1921
—*God of the Witches*. London, 1931
NOTESTEIN, W.—*History of Witchcraft in England 1558-1718*. Washington, 1911
PEEL, E. & SOUTHERN, P.—*The Trials of the Lancashire Witches*. New York, 1969
RANDOLPH, Vance—*Ozark Superstitions*. New York, 1947
SETH, Ronald—*Children Against Witches*. New York, 1969
SPRENGER & KRAMER—*Malleus Maleficarum*. London, 1928
STARKEY, Marion—*The Devil in Massachusetts*. New York 1949
STEIGER. Brad.—*Sex and Satanism*. N Y 1969
ST. LEGER-GORDON, Ruth—*The Witchcraft and Folklore of Dartmoor*. London, 1965
VALIENTE, Doreen—*Where Witchcraft Lives*. London, 1962
WILLIAMS, Charles—*Witchcraft*. London, 1941

QUEEN VICTORIA PRESS

Fiction by Raymond Buckland

A MISTAKE THROUGH THE HEART Book Three of the Bram Stoker mysteries (Books One and Two were published by Penguin/Random House's Berkley Prime Crime imprint)

CHURCHILL'S SECRET SPY WWII espionage novel

THE PENNY COURT ENQUIRERS Victorian mystery series
- *ONE CLUE AT A TIME* Book One
- *THE NOBLE SAVAGE* Book Two
- *DEADLY SPIRIT* Book Three

OUT OF THIS WORLD science fiction short story collection

PARANORMAL POETRY Poetry, strange and unusual

LAFF WITH OLAF A mixed bag of cartoons

In preparation:
- *THE WIITIKO INHERITANCE*
- *THE SECRET LIFE OF MISS EMMELINE CROMWELL*

Non-fiction by Raymond Buckland

WITCHCRAFT REVEALED An examination of Witchcraft and Wicca

OUIJA CONNECTION TO SPIRIT The Talking Board and how to contact the Spirit World

PARANORMAL PRIMER "How-to" on many popular metaphysical practices

HERE IS THE OCCULT An introduction to the wide world of the paranormal

THE BOOK OF ALCHEMY (plus CARDS and coloring book)

In preparation:
- *PSYCHIC WORLD SECRETS*
- *ANATOMY OF THE PARANORMAL*

Fiction by Eileen Lizzie Wells

FLETCHER'S FOLLY A Gothic romance mystery **In preparation:**

THE POSTMISTRESS MYSTERY

DESIGNING WOMEN

www.ingramcontent.com/pod-product-compliance
Lightning Source LLC
Chambersburg PA
CBHW020930090426
42736CB00010B/1099